The *Sarashina nikki*

First edition, 2020
Second, revised edition, 2023

Originally published in *Diaries of Court Ladies of Old Japan*

Published by TOYO PRess
Visit us at: **www.toyopress.com**

ISBN 978-94-92722-294

HEIAN COURT HEROINES

The *Sarashina nikki*

Sugawara no Takasue no Musume

Translated by

ANNIE SHEPLEY ŌMORI AND KŌCHI DOI

Edited and revised by

WILLIAM DE LANGE

HEIAN KYŌ

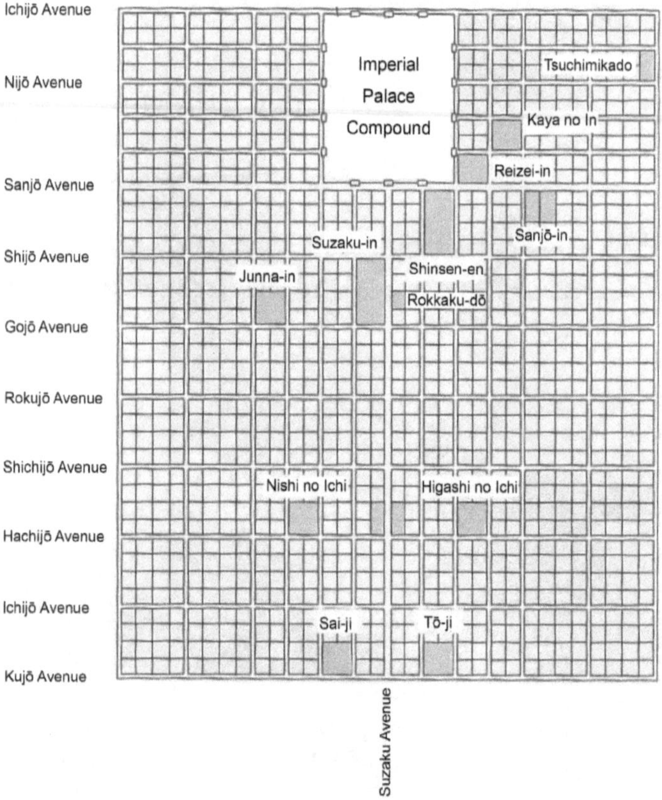

Ichijō Avenue
Nijō Avenue
Sanjō Avenue
Shijō Avenue
Gojō Avenue
Rokujō Avenue
Shichijō Avenue
Hachijō Avenue
Ichijō Avenue
Kujō Avenue
Imperial
Palace
Compound
Tsuchimikado
Kaya no In
Reizei-in
Sanjō-in
Suzaku-in
Junna-in
Shinsen-en
Rokkaku-dō
Nishi no Ichi
Higashi no Ichi
Sai-ji
Tō-ji
Suzaku Avenue

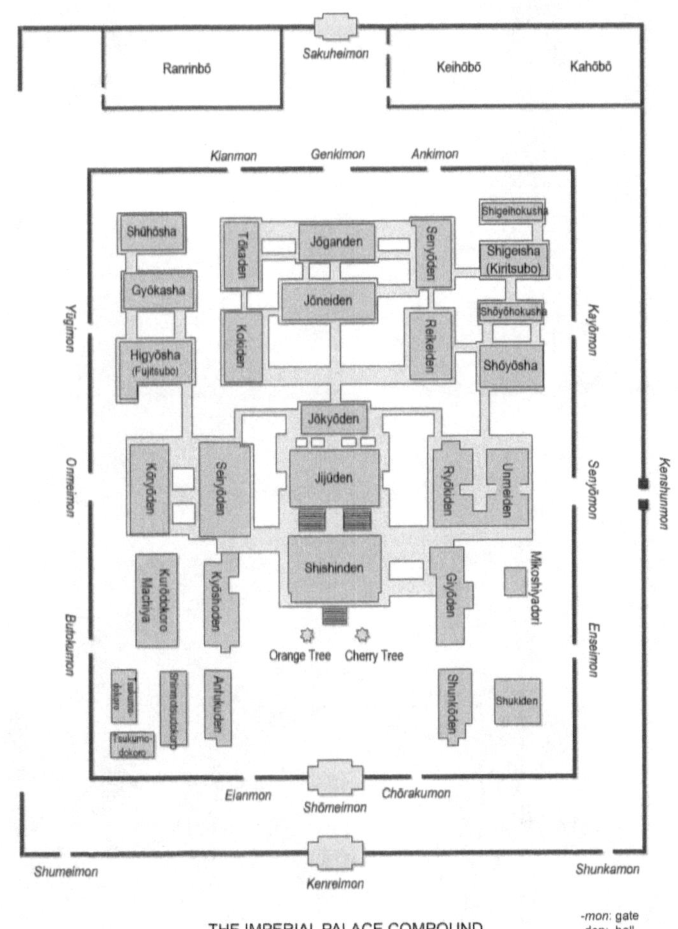

THE IMPERIAL PALACE COMPOUND

-*mon*: gate
-*den*: hall

Kazusa kokufu
Takeshiba
Nishitomi
Morokoshi
Tago no Ura
Numajiri
Takashi
Nogami
Narumi
Shikasu
Inugami
Kurumoto
Ōsaka
KYOTO
Uji
Nara
Sumiyoshi
Yoshino

Introduction

The Japanese have a convenient method of calling their historical periods by the names of the places which were the seats of government while they lasted. The first of these epochs of real importance is the Nara period, which began A.D. 710 and endured until 794; all before that may be classed as archaic. Previous to the Nara period, the Japanese had been a semi-nomadic race. As each successive emperor came to the throne, he built himself a new palace and founded a new capital. There had been more than sixty capitals before the Nara period. Such shifting was not conducive to the development of literature and the arts, and it was not until a permanent government was established at Nara, that these began to flourish. This is scarcely the place to trace the history of Japanese literature, but fully to understand these charming diaries of court ladies of old Japan, it is necessary to know a little of the world they lived in, to be able to feel their atmosphere and recognize their allusions.

We know a good deal about Japan today, but the Japan with which we are familiar only slightly resembles that of the diaries. Centuries of feudalism, of Dark Ages, have come between. We must go behind all this and begin again. We have all heard of the Forty-seven *Rōnin* and the *nō* drama, of *shōgun, daimyō,* and *samurai,* and many of us live in daily communion with Japanese prints. It gives us pause to reflect that the earliest of these things is almost as many centuries ahead of the ladies as it is behind us. *Shōgun* means simply "general," and of course there were always generals, but the power of the *shōgun,* and the military feudalism of which the *daimyō* and their attendant *samurai* were a part, did not really begin until the middle of the twelfth century and did not reach its full development until the middle of the fourteenth. The *nō* drama started with the ancient religious pantomimic dance, the *kagura,* but not until words were added in the fourteenth century did it become the *nō*. Similarly, block color printing was first practiced in 1695, while such famous print artists as Utamaro, Hokusai, and Hiroshige are all products of the eighteenth or early nineteenth centuries. To find the ladies behind the dark military ages, we must go back a long way, even to the century before their own, and so gain a sort of perspective for them and their time.

Chinese literature and civilization were introduced into Japan somewhere between 270 and 310 AD, and Buddhism followed in 552. Of course, all such dates must be taken with a certain degree of latitude; Oriental historians are anything but precise in these matters. Chinese influence and Buddhism are the two enormous facts to be reckoned with in understanding Japan, and considering what an effect they have had, it is not a little singular that Japan has always been able to preserve her native character. To be sure, Shintōism was never displaced by Buddhism, but the latter made a tremendous appeal to the Japanese temperament, as the diaries show. In fact, it was not until the Meiji period (1867-1912) that Shintōism was again made the state religion. With the introduction of Chinese civilization came the art of writing, when is not accurately known, but printing from movable blocks followed from Korea in the eighth century. As was inevitable under the circumstances, Chinese came to be considered the language of learning. Japanese scholars wrote in Chinese. All the "serious" books—history, theology, science, law—were written in Chinese as a matter of course. But, in 712, a volume called *Kojiki*, or *Records of Ancient Matters*, was compiled in the native tongue. It is the earliest book in Japanese now extant.

If the scholars wrote in a borrowed language, the poets knew better. They wrote in their own, and the poetry of the Nara period has been preserved for us in an anthology, the *Manyōshū* or *Collection of Ten Thousand Leaves*. This was followed at the beginning of the tenth century by the *Kokinshū*, the *Collection from Ancient and Modern Times*, to which the editor, Tsurayuki, felt obliged to write a Chinese preface. The ladies of the diaries were extremely familiar with these volumes, their own writings are full of allusions to poems contained in them. Sei Shōnagon, writing early in the eleventh century, describes a young lady's education as consisting of writing, music, and the twenty volumes of the *Kokinshū*. So it came about that while learned gentlemen still continued to write in Chinese, poetry, fiction, diaries, and desultory essays called *zuihitsu* (following the pen) were written in Japanese.

Now the position of women at this time was very different from what it afterward became in the feudal period. The Chinese called Japan the "Empress Country," because of the ascendancy which women enjoyed there. They were educated, they were allowed a share of the inheritance, and they had their own houses. It is an extraordinary and important fact that much of Japan's best literature has been written by women. Three of these most remarkable women are the authors of the diaries; a fourth to be named with them, Sei Shōnagon, to whom I have just referred, was a contemporary.

In 794, the capital was moved from Nara to Kyoto, which was given the name of Heian-kyō or "City of Peace," and with the removal, a new period, the Heian, began. It lasted until 1186, and our ladies lived in the very middle of it.

By this time Japan was thoroughly civilized; she was, indeed, a little over-civilized, a little too fined down and delicate. At least this is true of all that life which centered around the court at Heian-kyō. To historians, the Heian period represents the rise and fall of the Fujiwara family. This powerful family had served the emperors from time out of mind as heads of the Shintō priests, and after the middle of the seventh century, they became ministers or prime ministers. An immense clan, they gradually absorbed all the civil offices in the kingdom, while the military offices were filled by the Taira and Minamoto clans. It was the rise of these last as the Fujiwara declined that eventually led to the rule of the *shōgun* and the long centuries of feudalism and civil war.

But in the middle of the Heian period the Fujiwara were very much everywhere. Most of those court ladies who were the authors of remarkable books were the daughters of governors of provinces, and that meant Fujiwaras to a greater or lesser degree. At that time polygamy flourished in Japan, and the family had grown to a prodigious size. Since a civil office meant a post for a Fujiwara, many of them were happily provided for, but they were so numerous that they outnumbered the legitimate positions and others had to be created to fill the demand. The court was full of persons of both sexes holding sinecures, with a great deal of time on their hands and nothing to do in it but write poetry—which they did exceedingly well—and attend the various functions prescribed by etiquette. Ceremonials were many and magnificent, and poetry writing became not only a game but a natural adjunct to every possible event.

The Japanese as a people are dowered with a rare and exquisite taste, and in the Heian period taste was cultivated to an amazing degree. Murasaki Shikibu records the astounding pitch to which it had reached in a passage in her diary. Speaking of the emperor's ladies at a court festivity, she says of the dress of one of them:

> One had a little fault in the color combination at the wrist opening. When she went before the royal presence to fetch something, the nobles and high officials noticed it. Afterward Lady Saisho regretted it deeply. It was not so bad—only one color was a little too pale.

That passage needs no comment; it is completely illuminating. It is a paraphrase of the whole era.

Heian-kyō was a little city, long one way by some seventeen thousand odd feet, or about three and a third miles, wide the other by fifteen thousand, or approximately another three miles, and it is doubtful if the space within the city wall was ever entirely covered by houses. The palace was built in the so-called Azumaya style, a form of architecture also followed in noblemen's houses. The roof, or rather roofs, for there were many buildings, was covered with bark, and, inside, the divisions into rooms were made by different sorts of moving screens. At the period of the diaries, the reigning emperor, Ichijō, had two wives: Sadako, the first empress (*kōgō*), was the daughter of a previous prime minister, Michitaka, a Fujiwara, of course; the other, Akiko, daughter of Michinaga, the prime minister of the diaries and a younger brother of Michitaka, was second empress (*chūgū*). These empresses each occupied a separate house in the palace. The Kokiden was the name of empress Sadako's house; the Fujitsubō the name of Empress Akiko's. The rivalry between these ladies was naturally great, and extended even to their entourage. Each strove to surround herself with ladies who were not only beautiful but learned. The bright star of Empress Sadako's court was Sei Shōnagon, the author of a remarkable book, the *Makura no sōshi* or *Pillow Sketches*, while Murasaki Shikibu held the same exalted position in Empress Akiko's court.

XIV

We are to imagine a court founded upon the Chinese model, but not nearly so elaborate—a brilliant assemblage of persons all playing about a restricted but very bright center. From it, the high officials went out to be governors of distant provinces; lesser ones followed them to minor posts. In spite of the distinction of such positions, distance and the inconvenience of traveling made the going a sort of laurelled banishment. These gentlemen left Heian-kyō with regret and returned with satisfaction. But the going, and the years of residence away, was one of the commonplaces of social life. Fujiwara though one might be, one often had to wait and scheme for an office, and the diaries contain more than one reference to such waiting and the bitter disappointment when the office was not up to expectation.

These functionaries traveled with a large train of soldiers and servants, but, with the best will in the world, these last could not make the journeys other than tedious and uncomfortable. Still there were alleviations, because of the very taste of which I have spoken. The scenery was often beautiful, and whether the traveler was the governor himself or his daughter, he noticed and delighted in it. The *Sarashina nikki*, for instance, is full of this appreciation of nature; "a beautiful beach onto which the waves were breaking and retreating," a river that "rushed by in a white-crested torrent, as if rice had been powdered into a thick stream." We need only think of the now so familiar wood-prints to be convinced of the accuracy of this picture:

> Out toward sea, the waves were very high, but toward the lagoon, we could see the waves rippling through the dense pine groves on the lagoon's dreary sandbanks, glistening like a myriad of precious stones, and seeming to swallow up the crests of the trees.

These journeys were mostly made on horseback, but there were other methods of progression, which were probably not always feasible for long distances. The nobles used various kinds of carriages drawn by one bullock, and there were also palanquins carried by bearers.

Not only the officials made journeys, all the world made them, to temples and shrines for the good of their souls. There are religious yearnings in all the diaries, and many emperors and gentlemen entered the priesthood, Michinaga among them. *Sūtra* recitation and incantation were ceaselessly performed at court. We can gain some idea of the almost fanatical hold Buddhism had over the educated mind by the fact that the Fujiwara family built such great temples as Gokuraku-*ji*, Hōkō-in, Jōmyō-*ji*, Muryōju-*ji*, etc. It is recorded that emperor Shirakawa, at a date somewhat subsequent to the diaries, made pilgrimages four times to Kumano, and during his visits there "worshipped 5470 painted Buddhas, 127 carved Buddhas sixteen feet high, 3150 Buddhas lifesized, 2930 carved Buddhas shorter than three feet, 21 pagodas, 446,630 miniature pagodas." A busy man truly, but the record does not mention what became of the affairs of state meanwhile. That this worship was by no means lip-devotion merely, any reader of the *Sarashina nikki* can see. That it was mixed with much superstition and a profound belief in dreams is also abundantly evident. But let us, for a moment, recollect the time. It will place the marvel of this old, careful civilization before us as nothing else can.

To be sure, Greece and Rome had been, but they had passed away, or at least their greatness had gone and apparently left no trace. While these Japanese ladies were writing, Europe was in the full blackness of her darkest ages.

Germany was founding the Holy Roman Empire of the German Nation, characteristically founding it with the mailed fist. Moorish civilization was at its height in Spain. Robert Capet was king of poor famine-scourged France. Ethelred the Unready was ruling in England and doing his best to keep off the Danes by payment and massacre. Later, while the *Sarashina nikki* was being written, emperor Canute was sitting in his armchair and giving orders to the sea. Curious, curious world! So far apart from the world of the diaries. And to think that even five hundred years later Columbus was sending letters into the interior of Cuba, addressed to the Emperor of Japan!

These diaries show us a world extraordinarily like our own, if very unlike in more than one important particular. The noblemen and women of Emperor Ichijō's court were poets and writers of genius, their taste as a whole has never been surpassed by any people at any time, but their scientific knowledge was elementary in the extreme. Diseases and conflagrations were frequent. In a space of fifty-one years, the royal palace burnt down eleven times. During the same period, there were four great pestilences, a terrible drought, and an earthquake. Robbers infested many parts of the countryside and were a constant fear to travelers and pilgrims. Childbirth was very dangerous. The scene of the birth of a child to Empress Akiko, with which Murasaki Shikibu's diary begins, shows us all its bitter horror. From page to page we share the writer's suspense, and with our greater knowledge, it is with a sense of wonder that we watch the empress's return to health.

Diseases and conflagrations are seldom more than episodes in a normal life lived under sane conditions, and it is because these diaries reflect the real life of these three ladies that they are important. The world they portray is in most ways quite as advanced as our own, and in some, much more so. Rice was the staple of food, and although Buddhistic sentiment seldom permitted people to eat the flesh of animals, they had an abundance of fish, which was eaten boiled, baked, raw, and pickled. There was no sugar, but cakes were made of fruit and nuts, and there was always rice wine or *sake*. Gentlefolk usually dressed in silk. They wore many layers of colored silk garments, and delighted in the harmony produced by the color combinations, or of a bright lining subdued by the tone of an outer robe. The ladies all painted their faces, and the whole toilet was a matter of sufficient moment to raise it into a fine art. Many of these lovely dresses are described by Murasaki Shikibu:

> The beautiful shape of their hair, tied with ribbons, was like that of the beauties in Chinese pictures. Lady Saemon held the emperor's sword. She wore a blue-green patternless *karaginu* and shaded train with floating bands and a belt of floating thread brocade dyed in dull red. Her outer robe was trimmed with five folds and was chrysanthemum colored. The glossy silk was of crimson. Her figure and movement, when we caught a glimpse of it, was flower-like and dignified. Lady Ben no Naishi held the box of the emperor's seals. Her *uchigi* was grape-colored. She is a very small and smile-giving person and seems shy and I was sorry for her.... Her hairbands were blue-green. Her appearance suggested one of the ancient dream maidens descended from heaven.

A little later she tells us that "the beaten stuffs were like the mingling of dark and light maple leaves in autumn." Describing in some detail the festivity at which these ladies appeared, she makes the comment that "only the right bodyguard wore clothes of shrimp pink." To one in love with color, these passages leave a deep nostalgia for such a bright and sophisticated court.

And everywhere, everywhere, there is poetry. A gentleman hands a lady a poem on the end of his fan and she is expected to reply in kind within the instant. Poems form an important part in the ritual of betrothal. A daughter of good family never allowed herself to be seen by men—a custom that appears to have admitted many exceptions. A man would write a poetical love letter to the lady of his choice which she must answer amiably, even should she have no mind to him. If she were happily inclined, he would visit her secretly at night and leave before daybreak. He would then write again, following which she would give a banquet and introduce him to her family. After this, he could visit her openly, although she would still remain for some time in her father's house. This custom of love letter writing and visiting is shown in Izumi Shikibu's diary. Obviously, the poems were short, and here, in order to understand those in the text, it may be well to consider for a moment what constitutes Japanese poetry.

Japanese is a syllabic language like our own, but, unlike our own, it is not accented. Also, every syllable ends with a vowel, the consequence being that there are only five rhymes in the whole language. Since the employment of so restricted a rhyme scheme would be unbearably monotonous, the Japanese hit upon the happy idea of counting syllables. Our metrical verse also counts syllables, but we combine them into different kinds of accented feet. Without accent, this was not possible, so the Japanese poet limits their number and uses them in a pattern of alternating lines. Their prosody is based upon the numbers five and seven, a five-syllable line alternating with one of seven syllables, with, in some forms, two seven-syllable lines together at the end of a period, in the manner of our couplet. The favorite form, the *tanka*, is in thirty-one syllables, and runs five, seven, five, seven, seven. There is a longer form, the *nagauta*, but it has never been held in as high favor. The poems in the diaries are all *tanka* in the original. It can be seen that much cannot be said in so confined a medium, but much can be suggested, and it is just in this art of suggestion that the Japanese excel. The *hokku* is an even briefer form. In it, the concluding hemistich of the *tanka* is left off, and it is just in his hemistich that the meaning of the poem is brought out, so that the *hokku* is a mere essence—a whiff of an idea to be created in full by the hearer. But the *hokku* was not invented until the fifteenth century. Before that, the *tanka*, in spite of occasional attempts to vary it by adding more lines, changing their order, using the pattern in combination as a series of stanzas, reigned supreme, and it is still the chief classic form for all Japanese poetry.

Unlike Murasaki Shikibu's famous diary, which is concerned with only a few years of her life, the *Sarashina nikki* covers a long period in the life of its author. The first part was written when she was twelve years old, the last entry was made when she was past fifty. It begins with a journey from Shimōsa to Heian-kyō along the Tōkaidō in 1021, which is followed by a second journey some years later from Heian-kyō to Sarashina, a place that has never been satisfactorily identified, although some critics have supposed it to have been in the province of Shinano. The rest of the diary consists of jottings at various times—accounts of books read, of places seen, of pilgrimages to temples, of records of dreams and portents, of communings with herself on life and death, of expressions of resignation and sorrow.

The book takes its name from the second of the journeys, *Sarashina nikki,* meaning simply "Sarashina diary," for, strangely enough, we do not know the author's name. We do know that she was the daughter of Fujiwara no Takasue, and that she was born in 1009. In 1017, Takasue was appointed governor of a province and went with his daughter to his new post. It is the return journey, made in 1021, with which the diary opens.

Takasue's daughter shared with so many of her contemporaries the deep love of nature and the power to express this love in words. I have already quoted one or two of her entries on this journey. We follow the little company over mountains and across rivers, we camp with them by night, and tremble as they trembled lest robbers should attack them. We see what the little girl saw:

The mountain range called Nishitomi looked like a wide folding screen decorated with splendid paintings. Toward one side, we saw a beautiful beach onto which the waves were breaking and retreating.

We share her disappointment when she says: "We passed a place called Eight Bridges. But it was only a name, there was no trace of a bridge and nothing to see of interest."

They reach Heian-kyō and a rather dull life begins, enlivened only by the avid reading of romances, among them the *Genji monogatari*. Then her sister dies giving birth to a child, and life becomes not only dull but sorrowful. After a time, she obtains a position at court, but neither her upbringing nor her disposition suited her for such a place. She mentions that her mother was "extremely old-fashioned," and it is evident that she had been taught to look inward rather than outward.

An abortive little love affair lightens her dreariness for a moment. Life dealt hardly with the sensitive girl: from year to year she grows more wistful, but suddenly something happens, a mere hint of a gleam, but opening a possibility of brightness. Who he was, we do not know, but she meets him on an evening when "sweet-voiced priests were reciting *sūtra* throughout the night." They talked and exchanged poems, but she does not meet him again until the next year. Then, after an evening entertainment to which she has not gone, she "opened the sliding doors to the corridor and looked out, and I saw the morning moon very faint and beautiful." And he is there. Again they exchange poems and she believes happiness has at last arrived. He is to come with his lute and sing to her. "I wanted to hear it," she writes, and how she "waited for the fit occasion, but it never came." A year later she has lost hope, she writes a poem and adds, "that was the end of it." Nothing more, indeed, but what is told conveys all the misery of her deceived longing.

The last part of the diary is concerned chiefly with accounts of pilgrimages and dreams. She marries (who and when is not recorded) and has children. Her husband dies, and with his death the spring of her life seems to have run dry. Her last entry is very sad: "My people went to live elsewhere and I lived alone in my solitary home." So we leave her, a beautiful, shy spirit who knew much sorrow.

Amy Lowell

Departure

I was brought up in Kazusa,[1] a distant province that, as the old song says, "lies farther than the farthest end of the eastern road."

I am ashamed to think how shabby I must have appeared in the eyes of cultured people then. Yet somehow I learned that there are such things as romances in the world and I wanted to read them. During daytime when there was nothing to do, or at night when we were sitting together, my elder sister or stepmother would tell me this or that story. Or they would relate the tale of the shining Prince Genji.[2] Hearing such fragments, I wanted to learn the whole story, but how could I expect them to recount these stories to me in their entirety by learning them by heart?

Disheartened, I had someone make me a life-sized image of Yakushi Buddha.[3] I would wash my hands and, when people were not looking, secretly go before the altar and pray to him with all my heart, bowing my head deep down to the floor, saying, "Please let me go to Heian-kyō. I hear there are many stories to be had there."

At the age of thirteen, Father's term in office expired and we had to return to Heian-kyō. On the 3rd of September, we temporarily moved to Imatachi while the old house where I had played as a child was completely dismantled and our servants busied themselves removing the furniture in preparation for our return.[4]

At sunset, in the foggy twilight, just as I was getting into the palanquin, I looked back at what had been my house and I beheld, standing all by itself, the Buddha before which I had furtively gone to pray—I was sorry and secretly shed tears at the thought of leaving him behind.

Our temporary dwelling was just a crude, thatched house, without a fence or even shutters, but we hung up *sudare* and curtains. And in the far-off distance, a wide plain stretched out toward the south.

On the east and west the sea crept close, lending grace to

the setting, which was further enhanced by the evening mists that drifted in from the sea. I would get up early in the mornings to take in the various views and regretted the thought of having to leave this place.

But on the 15th of the same month, while it was raining so hard that it grew dark, we crossed the border between Kazusa and Shimōsa and spent the night at a place called Ikada. It was raining so hard that our lodging was almost submerged. I was so afraid I could not sleep. I saw only three lone trees standing on a little hill in the waste. The next day we spent drying our drenched clothes and in waiting for those who had remained behind in Kazusa to wind things up to catch up with us and join us.

White Sands

On the seventeenth, we started early in the morning. Long ago, there lived in Shimōsa a man by the name of Mano no Chō.[5] He had thousands and thousands of rolls of cloth woven and had them bleached in the river that now flows over the place where his great mansion stood. Four of the large gate posts remained and protruded from the middle of the river.

Hearing people sing songs about the place, I wrote:

> *Had I not seen erect in the river*
> *These solid timbers of the olden time*
> *How could I know, how could I feel*
> *The story of that house?*

That evening we lodged at Kuroto no Hama.[6] White sand stretched far toward the vast mountains in the distance. The pinewoods were dense, the moon above was bright, and the sound of the wind made me feel lonely. The others were charmed and eulogized the place, and I too wrote a poem:

> *For this night only*
> *The autumn moon*
> *At Kuroto no Hama*
> *Shall shine for me,*
> *For this night only!*
> *—I cannot sleep.*

The Wetnurse

Early in the morning we left Kuroto no Hama and came to the Futoi River,[7] on the border between Shimōsa and Musashi. We lodged at the ferry of Matsusato, near the Kagami rapids, while all night long our luggage was being ferried across the river.

It was at Matsusato that my wetnurse, who had lost her husband, gave birth to a child so that we had to go up to Heian-kyō separately.[8] I missed her terribly and wanted to go and see her, so my elder brother brought me to her in his arms.

Though the others referred to the place where we were staying as a temporary hunting lodging, at least it had curtains to keep out the wind; while the hut in which the wet-

nurse was forced to stay without her husband was a course and primitive hovel with just one mat by way of roofing, so that the moonlight lit up its every corner. Seeing her lying there, with the bright moonlight shining down on her tortured shape huddled under a crimson garment, she seemed so white and pure—far above any ordinary wetnurse.

She had not seen me for some time and, surprised to see me, she wept as she stroked my face. I found it hard to abandon her there so pitilessly, and could not help feeling at a loss when my brother took me back in a hurry. Even after I had left her, her image haunted me, which made me sad and I went to bed that night feeling deflated, unable to find any diversion in gazing at the moon.

The next morning, our palanquins were loaded into a boat and we crossed the Futoi River. Having unloaded and assembled the palanquins on the opposite shore, those who had come with us to see us off returned home. We, who were going up to Heian-kyō, stayed there for a while. As it was a parting for life, all of us—both those who stayed and those who returned—wept. And even I in my childlike mind felt a deep sense of sadness.

The Princess

We were now in the province of Musashi. There was no charm in this place. The sand of the beaches was not white but like mud. People praise the purple grass that grows on the plains of Musashi, but it was only a waste of reeds and grass, which grew so high that we could not see the bows of our horsemen who were forcing their way through the tall grass. Passing through the plain of reeds I saw a ruined temple called Takeshiba-*dera*.

We came across the foundation stones of a mansion that once went by the name of Hahasō. When I asked, "What place is this?" they answered, "In the old days, this place was called Takeshiba. A local from here was presented to the emperor's palace by the governor as a guard to keep the watch-fire. He was once sweeping the garden in front of a princess's room and singing:

Ah, me! Ah, me!
My weary doom to labor here in the palace!
Seven good wine bottles have I—three in my province.
There where they stand I have hung straight-stemmed
Gourds of the finest—
They turn to the west when the east wind blows,
They turn to the east when the west wind blows,
They turn to the North when the south wind blows,
They turn to the south when the North wind blows.
And there I sit watching them
Turning and turning forever—
Oh, my gourds! Oh, my wine bottles!

"Thus he was muttering to himself when, a princess, the emperor's favorite daughter, was sitting alone behind the *misu*. She came forward and, leaning against the doorpost, listened to the man singing. She was very interested in the gourds and how they were turning and wanted to see them. She was so fascinated by the gourds, that she pushed up the blind called the guard, saying, 'Man, come here!' The man heard it very respectfully, and with great reverence drew near the balustrade. 'Tell me again what you have been saying.' And he told her about the wine bottles 'I must go and see them,' she said, 'I have my own reason for saying so.'

"He felt great awe, but assuming it was his karma from a former life, he lifted her on his back and carried her back to his province of Musashi. He feared that men would pursue them, and that night, reaching the Seta Bridge, he set the princess down and broke away the planks between the pillars. Then, bounding over the gap with the princess on his back, he arrived at his native place after seven days' and seven nights' journey.

"The emperor and empress were greatly surprised when they found the princess was lost and began to search for her. Someone said, 'The guard from Musashi ran off carrying something with an exquisite fragrance on his back. We have been looking for them but have not found a trace of them.'

They assumed the guard would have gone back home and sent imperial messengers down to Musashi to pursue them, but when they got to the Seta Bridge they found its planks missing and were unable to cross.

Three months had passed by the time the messenger reached Musashi and asked for the princess. The princess called the messengers to her and said, 'I believe it is fate that has brought me here. I wanted to see the man's home and told him to bring me here, and so he did. And I have found this place a very pleasant place to live. If this man were punished and whipped, what should I do? It must be my karma from a previous life that I am to leave my descendants in this province—please hurry back to the capital and tell the emperor so!'

"Informed by the messenger the emperor declared, 'It cannot be helped. Even if I were to punish the man, I cannot bring back the princess. As long as that man of Takeshiba lives I cannot give Musashi province to him, or let him levy any taxes. But I will entrust the province to the princess.'

"Thus it was that, in accordance with the Emperor's decree, a palace was built in this place and that the princess was allowed to live here.

"After the princess passed away, the palace was made into

a temple by the name of Takeshiba. And the descendants of the princess took on the family name of Musashi. After that, the guards of the watchfire were always women."

The Singers

We waded through a waste of common reed and silver grass and reached the Asuda River, the border between Musashi and Sagami,[9] It is the river Where Ariwara no Narihira composed his famous poem, *Tell me One Thing*.[10] In the book of his poetical works the river is called the Sumida River.

We crossed the river in a boat and entered the province of Sagami. The mountain range called Nishitomi looked like a wide folding screen decorated with splendid paintings. Toward one side, we saw a beautiful beach onto which the waves were breaking and retreating.

At Morokoshigahara, it took us two to three days to cross the dazzlingly white sands.

A man said, "During the summer, the *Yamato Nadeshiko*[11] bloom in deep and light shades, like a brocade blanket. We are now at the end of autumn so you cannot see them." Still, I saw some pinks scattered about blooming pitiably. They said, "It is funny that the *Yamato Nadeshiko* should be blooming here at Morokoshigahara."[12]

Four or five days before we reached it, Mount Ashigara loomed dark and foreboding in the distance. And even at its base, we could only occasionally glimpse the sky, so unspeakably dense were the trees growing on its slopes.

We lodged in a hut at the foot of the mountain. It was a dark moonless night, and I felt swallowed up and lost in the darkness, when three women of pleasure came out of somewhere. One was about fifty years old, the second twenty, and the third about fourteen or fifteen.

We sat them down in front of our lodging and a *karakasa* was unfolded for them. My servant lighted a fire so that we could see them. They said that they were the grandchildren of a certain Kohata. They had very long hair that hung over their foreheads. Their faces were white and clean, and they seemed rather like maids serving at the house of a nobleman. They had clear, sweet voices, and their beautiful singing reached to the heavens. All were charmed and, taking great interest, came nearer. Someone said, "The singers of the western provinces are not as splendid as this," and at this the singers closed their song with the words, "Compared to the women of pleasure from Naniwa, we don't amount to much."[13]

They were handsome and neatly dressed, with voices of rare beauty. And yet, these women wandered off into those fearful mountains again, causing those who remained behind to weep with regret. And I too, in my child's mind, was reluctant to leave this lodging and its singers.

The next morning, while it was still dark, we crossed Mount Ashigara. Even at its foot the woods were dense, and all the more so as were entered the mountains. Words cannot express my fear in the midst of it. Clouds rolled beneath our feet and it felt as if I was treading on them.

Halfway up the mountain, there was a clearing below the trees where there grew some wild ginger.[14] We all praised it saying, "How strange that they should grow here among the mountains, so far from the human world." We encountered as many as three rivers among the mountains.

Having crossed the mountains with great difficulty, we

arrived at the barrier of Yokoashi. Beyond here lay the province of Suruga. Near the barrier lies Iwatsubo. There was an indescribably large square rock through a hole in which very cold and utterly pure water came rushing forth.

Mount Fuji

We were now the province of Mount Fuji. From Kazusa where I was brought up, I could see the mountain toward the west. There is no mountain like it in the whole wide world. It soars in hues of deep blue and is covered with eternal snow so that it looks as if it wears a dress of deep violet covered with a white robe. Smoke rose from a little level place at its summit, and at night we even saw fire.

We arrived at the Kiyomi barrier near the sea. There was a multitude of huts and a fence of stakes driven into the ground right up to the shore. The smoke from the mountain, the smoke from the huts, and the spray of the sea—all drifted together to make it look as if the waves at Kiyomi were even taller. I had not seen anything as beautiful as this!

The waves at Tago no Ura were so high that we had to row out to sea by boat.[15]

There was a ferry at the Ōi River, where the river's waters rushed by in a white-crested torrent, as if rice had been powdered into a thick stream, unlike anything I had ever seen in this world.

As for the Fuji River, it comes tumbling down from Mount Fuji. A local came up to us and told me the following story:

"Around a year ago, as I was setting out from home, it was a very hot day, and I was resting on the bank of this river when I saw something yellow come floating down toward me. It caught on something and was stopped in its tracks. I picked it up and found it was a scrap of paper with words written on it in thick and clear red characters. Puzzled, I read what it said and found it was a list of the governors to be appointed to the various provinces next year, including the new governor for this province of Suruga. But then I saw that next to it was the name of a second person. Intrigued, I took the piece of paper with me, dried it, and put it away. The following year, when the governors were being appointed, I found that all the names listed on the slip of paper were correct, and so was the name of the governor appointed for this province. But within three months, the new governor passed away and the name of his replacement turned out to be the same as that written in the margins. There are such things. I think that the gods assemble on Mount Fuji this year to settle next year's affairs."

Eight Bridges

We passed the Ōi River at Numajiri without trouble, but I fell so ill when we entered Tōtōmi Province that I did not even notice we crossed the pass of Sayo no Nakayama. I was quite exhausted, so when we came to the bank of the Tenryū River, we built a temporary dwelling and passed several days there. And at length, I got better.

The winter had set in and the wind from the river blew hard and the cold became intolerable. After crossing the river we went toward the bridge at Hamana. When we went down east on Father's appointment as governor, there had been a bridge made of logs with their bark still attached. But now we could not find even a trace of it, so we had to cross the lagoon by boat.

Out toward sea, the waves were very high, but toward the lagoon, we could see the waves rippling through the dense pine groves on the lagoon's dreary sandbanks, glistening like a myriad of precious stones, and seeming to swallow up the crests of the trees. It was a beautiful sight.

We went on and crossed Inohana Hill—an unspeakably weary ascent it was—and reached Takashi, on the shore of Mikawa Province. We passed a place called Eight Bridges.[16] But it was only a name, there was no trace of a bridge and nothing to see of interest.

That evening, we built a shelter under a tall persimmon tree among the Futamura Hills. The whole night persimmons kept falling on the roof of our shelter and people picked them up.

It was already late October by the time we passed Mount Miyaji, yet the red maple leaves had not yet fallen and were at their peak:

> *Furious mountain winds in their passing*
> *Must spare this spot*
> *For red maple leaves are clinging*
> *Even yet to the branch.*

On the border between Mikawa and Owari, we took the Shikasuga ferry, which is a play on the words "As expected," which is very amusing.[17]

Buddha

When we passed the bay of Narumi in the province of Owari, the evening tide was coming in, and we feared that if it came any higher we would not be able to cross. So in a panic we ran as fast as we could.

At the border of Mino we took the ferry at Sunomata and arrived at Nogami, where women of pleasure came out and sang for us all night. They reminded me of the singers we had met at Ashigara and I thought of them longingly.

It now began to snow and I did not take any interest when we crossed the Fuwa barrier and Mount Atsumi in a blinding storm. In the province of Omi we stayed four or five days at the house of a man called Okinaga.

At the foot of Mount Mitsusaka, hail and rain fell all day

and all night without even a ray of sunshine; it was terribly gloomy. Setting out from there, we somehow made it past Inugami, Kanzaki, Yasu, and Kurumoto.

It was wonderful to see the waters of Lake Biwa stretched out far into the distance, where I caught occasional glimpses of Nade and Chikubu Islands. The Seta bridge had entirely collapsed and we had great difficulty crossing the river.[18]

We made a stop at Awazu, and arrived at Heian-kyō on the second day of December, the month of the Running Priests.

We planned to arrive in the capital after it had grown dark and set out again at the hour of the Monkey.[19] When we reached the Ōsaka barrier, my eye fell on the face of a six feet tall roughly-hewn Buddha that protruded from above a course fence. Serene and indifferent to its surroundings, it just stood there in that deserted place, making me all the more grateful when I passed it by at a distance.

We had traveled through many provinces but the barriers at Kiyomigata and Ōsaka were the most splendid.

It was well after dark when we arrived at our house just west of the Sanjō Palace.

Books

Our garden was very wide and wild with great, fearful trees not inferior to those I had seen among the mountains we had come through, and it was difficult to believe we were actually in the capital. Yet I found it hard to settle in. Though I was quite busy with other things, I continually pestered Mother saying, "Please give me books to read! Please give me books to read!"
A relative of Mother's by the name of Emon no Myōbu, happened to be a lady-in-waiting to the princess of the Sanjō Palace.[20] And when I visited her and wrote to her, she took interest in my curious passion and gladly sent me some excellent bound books in the lid of a lacquered writing box, saying that these copies had been given to her by

the princess. My joy knew no bounds and I read them day and night. I soon began to wish for more stories, but as I was an utter stranger to Heian-kyō, who could I turn to in order to provide me with them?

Plum Tree

My stepmother,[21] had once been a lady-in-waiting at court. But when Father had gone down to Kazusa, she had become disappointed, reproachful, and left him, taking their five-year-old son with her. On her departure she had told me, "I will never forget how kind you have been to me." And pointing to a huge plum tree growing close to the eave of our house, she said, "I will come and visit you again when the tree is in flower." I longed for her return and wept quietly as the year drew to a close.

I spent my days looking at the plum tree thinking, *Come on, plum tree, bloom! Stepmother said she would return when you do!* But at the same time I wondered, *Will she?*

At length the tree came into flower, but there was no

word of my stepmother, and breaking off a blossom, I sent it to her with the words:

> You gave me words of hope,
> Are they not long delayed?
> Even spring has not forgotten the tree,
> Though it was withered with frost.

She wrote back tenderly:

> Wait, and don't lose hope,
> The blossom fragrance will herald
> The arrival of someone unexpected.

The Story of Genji

That spring the world was disquieted by pestilence. My wetnurse, who had filled my heart with pity on that moonlight night at the ford of Matsuzato, died on the first day of March. I lamented hopelessly without any way to set my mind at ease, and even forgot my passion for romances.

I passed day after day weeping bitterly, and when I first looked out of doors again, I saw the evening sun on cherry blossoms all falling in confusion:

> *Flowers are falling, yet I may see them again*
> *When spring returns.*
> *But, oh, my longing for my wetnurse*
> *Who has departed from us forever!*

I also learned that the daughter of Dainagon Fujiwara no Yukinari,[22] the emperor's chamberlain, had passed away. I sympathized with her husband, the lieutenant-general, all the more, for I was deeply grieving myself.

When I had first arrived at the capital I had been given a book of the handwriting of this noble lady for my copy-book. In it were written several poems, among them the following:

> *When you see the smoke*
> *Floating up the valley of Toribe Hill,[23]*
> *Then you will understand me,*
> *Who seemed shadow-like even when alive.*

I looked at these poems, written in such beautiful handwriting, and I shed more tears. Seeing me absorbed in grief like this, Mother troubled herself to console me. She searched for romances and when she gave them to me, she indeed found that I was naturally consoled.

I read the *Genji monogatari*'s chapter about Lady Wakamurasaki and longed to read the book's other chapters,[24] but as I was still a stranger in the capital I had no way of finding them. Impatient and yearning to read more I prayed within my heart of hearts, *Please let me read this* Story of Genji *from the first chapter to the last!*

Even when I went to pray with my parents at the temple at Uzumasa,[25] all I asked for was to be able to read this story as soon as we got home, but it was all in vain.

Lamenting my disappointment, I one day visited my aunt, who had recently come up from the country. She showed a tender interest in me and lovingly said, "You have grown up beautifully."

As I was about to leave, she said, "What shall I give you? You will not be interested in serious things: I will give you what you like best." And she gave me more than fifty chapters of the *Genji monogatari* in a wooden case, as well as the *Ise monogatari*, the *Yojimi*, the *Serikawa*, the *Shirara*, and the *Asauzu*. How happy I was when I came home carrying all these books in a bag! Until then I had only read a volume here and there, unable to read the whole story. Now I could lie down behind a screen without being a burden to others and read the whole *Genji monogatari*, from the very first chapter. To be a empress was nothing compared to this!

All day and all night I read as late as I could keep my eyes open, setting a lamp close beside me. As I did nothing else but read, I had soon memorized the words and thought it a splendid thing that they came to me.

Once I had a vivid dream of a very dashing priest in a yellow stole who came to me and said, "Learn the fifth book of the *Hokekkyō* at once." I did not tell anyone about the dream, nor had I any mind to study the *Hokekkyō*, but continued to indulge in my romances. I was not a beauty but believed that with time I would grow beautiful beyond compare, with long, long, flowing hair, like the Shining Prince Genji's Lady Yugao, or like Lady Ukifune, the lover of Master Kaoru, the general of Uji. When I think of it now, I am shocked at how foolish I was then.

Our Garden

On the first day of May, the Rice Sprout month, I saw the white petals of the Tachibana orange tree that grew near the eaves of our house covering the ground:

> *Scarce had my mind received with wonder;*
> *The thought of newly fallen snow—*
> *Seeing the ground lie white—*
> *When the scent of Tachibana flowers*
> *Arose from fallen blossoms.*

In our garden trees grew as thick as in the dark forest of Ashigara, and in the month of October, the Month of the Gods,[26] its red leaves were more beautiful than those of the surrounding mountains, like a brocade covering. A visitor from outside the capital said, "On my way here I passed a place where red leaves were beautiful"; and I improvised:

> *No sight can be more autumnal*
> *Than that of our garden*
> *Tenanted by an autumnal person*
> *Weary of the world!*

Since I still spent my days dreaming about romances and continued to fill my thoughts until I fell asleep at night, I dreamt of a man who said, "I have built a stream in the gardens of the Rokkaku-dō[27] on behalf of the princess of the first rank, the daughter of the empress dowager."

When I asked him why he had done so, he said, " "Pray to the heaven-illuminating goddess Amaterasu." But even though I saw such dreams at night, I did not tell anyone about them, nor did I give them any further thought. What else could I do?

When spring came, I spent my days going up to the gardens of the princess of the first rank, gazing at them, and writing:

Cherry-blossoms waited for—
Cherry-blossoms lamented over—
As if her gardens were mine.

Blossoms

Toward the end of March, I moved to someone else's house to avoid the evil influence of the earth god.[28] There I saw delightful cherry blossoms still on the tree, and the day after my return home I sent this poem:

> *Alone, without tiring,*
> *I gazed at the cherry-blossoms of your garden.*
> *The spring was closing—they were about to fall*

Whenever the flowers came and went, I could think of nothing but those days when my nurse died, and sadness descended upon me, which grew even deeper when I read the writings of the deceased princess of the first rank.

The Cat

Once in May, as I was up late reading a romance, I heard a cat mewing with a long-drawn-out cry. I looked up in surprise and saw an adorable cat. When I tried to find out where it had come from, my sister said, "Be quiet! Don't tell anybody. It is a darling cat and we will keep it." So we kept the cat with us.

We thought that someone might come looking for the cat and kept the cat hidden. She would just sit there with me and my sister, never visit the servants' quarters and turn her face away from unclean food and refuse to eat it.

It was while we were thus tenderly looking after our cat, that my sister fell ill and that, the whole household being in a state, the cat was shut up in the house's northern wing.

She began to cry loudly and make a racket but I thought it better to keep her there when my ill sister got up and said, "Where is she—the cat? Bring her here!"

I asked her why, and she said: "I dreamt the cat came to me and said, 'I am the reincarnation of the daughter of the chamberlain chief councilor. Having been close in my previous life, your sister took pity on me so that I stayed here. But now I have been shut up in the servants' quarters, I am very miserable.' Saying this, the cat wept bitterly and looked like a noble and beautiful person, and when I woke up I realized it was the cat crying!"

After that, we never locked the cat up in the northern wing again and took great care of her.

Once, when I was sitting alone, the cat came to me and, stroking her head, I said, "You are the daughter of the chamberlain chief councilor, aren't you? I will have to tell your father so." She looked at me intently and miaowed softly. It may be my fancy, but as I was watching her she seemed no common cat. She seemed to understand what I was saying, making me love her all the more.

Fire

I had heard that a certain person possessed a book based on the epic Chinese poem the *Chang hen ge,* the *Song of Everlasting Regret.*[29] I longed to read it, but I was too shy to say so.

On the seventh day of the seventh month I found a happy means to send the suggestion of my wish:

> *This is the night when in the ancient Past,*
> *The Herder Star embarked to meet the Weaving One;*
> *In its sweet remembrance, the wave rises*
> *High in the River of Heaven.*
> *Likewise swells my heart to see the famous book.*

The reply came:

The star gods meet on the shore of the Heavenly River,
Like theirs full of ecstasy is my heart
And grave things of daily life are forgotten
On the night your message comes to me.

On the thirteenth day of that month, the moon shone very brightly, chasing darkness away from every corner of the heavens.

At midnight, while everyone else was fast asleep, my sister and I went out onto the veranda and, gazing thoughtfully at the heavens, she said, "If I flew away now, leaving no trace behind, what would you think of it?" She saw that her words shocked me, and she turned the conversation lightly to other things, and we laughed.

Then I heard a carriage with a runner before it stop near the house. The man in the carriage called out, "Ogi no Ha! Ogi no Ha!" twice, but no woman made a reply. The man called in vain until he grew tired. Then he began to play most elegantly on his flute until the carriage eventually drove away:

Flute music in the night,
Like the sighing autumn wind,
Why does Ogi no Ha not reply?

Chiming in, my sister replied:

Alas! The autumn wind sadly moved on,
Without caring to wait
For Ogi no Ha's reply.

We sat together looking up into the firmament and went to bed after daybreak.

One night in April of the following year, a fire broke out, and the cat we believed to be the daughter of the chamberlain chief councilor and had grown so fond of that we lovingly called her such and which had been waited on accordingly was burned to death. She had been used to come mewing whenever I called out, "Daughter of the Master Chief Councilor!" as if she understood me. Even Father would say, "What a strangely sad thing! I should report this to the chief councilor." How pitiful it was that we should have lost her in this way.

The gardens of our old house had been wide and wild like the uninhabited mountains, and when the cherries blossomed or the maple leaves turned red, it was in no way inferior to the surrounding mountains.

Having grown fond of our old garden, I found the new one incomparably small—too small to be called a garden, really, without any trees, which made me very sad.

In the garden of the house opposite ours', white and red plum blossoms grew in confusion and their perfume drifted over on the wind:

> *From the neighboring garden,*
> *The fragrant air*
> *Fills my soul with longing*
> *For the plum tree*
> *Under the eaves of our old house.*

Corpse

On the first day of May, my sister died giving birth to a
child. From childhood, even a stranger's death had upset
me greatly and would affect me for a long time afterward.
How much more, then, was I struck by the death of my
own sister!

While mother and the others were with my sister in the
room where they were holding the wake, I lay with the
children she had left behind, one on either side of me. The
moonlight found its way through one of the cracks in the
dilapidated roof and fell on the face of one of them, which
sight gave my heart such a deep a jolt that I covered the
child's face with my sleeve, while I drew the other child
closer to me as I lay worrying.

When the period of mourning had passed, a relative sent a book titled *The Prince Who Searched for a Corpse*,[30] with a note saying:

> *Your elder sister implored me to get a hold of this book*
> *and send it to her, which I am now doing. How sad that*
> *she should have passed away without having seen it.*

I replied:

> *What reason can there be that she*
> *Strangely should seek a romance of corpse?*
> *Buried now is the seeker*
> *Deep under the mosses.*

My sister's wetnurse said, "There is no reason for me to stay on any longer," and went back home weeping.

> *Thus death or parting*
> *Separates us each from the other,*
> *Why must we part?*
> *Oh, world too sad for me!*

*I would like you to stay on, if only as a memento to my
elder sister! I can write no more, for the inkstone's water
had frozen and I have run out of words and courage.*

How shall I gather memories of my sister?
The stream of letters is congealed.
No comfort may be found in icicles.

So I wrote to the nurse, and she wrote back:

Like a plover on the beach
Soon to be washed away,
Unable to leave an enduring trace
In this fleeting world.

The nurse went to see my elder sister's grave and re-
turned home sobbing. And I wrote:

I seek her in the field, but she is not there,
Nor does she linger in the smoke.
Where is her last abode?

When my stepmother heard this she wrote:

Ignorant of her last abode,
All you had to guide you
Were the tears you shed along the way.

The person who had sent the book titled *The Prince Who Searched for a Corpse* wrote:

How she must have wandered seeking the unfindable
In the unfamiliar fields of bamboo grasses,
Vainly weeping!

Reading these poems, my brother, who had conducted my sister's funeral that night, wrote:

Even as we watched
The pyre's smoke arose and died again.
How could she have ever reached
The bamboo grassed of the plain?

Afterward, it snowed for many days on end, and I thought

of the nun who lived on Mount Yoshino, and I wrote to her
saying:

> *Now the snow is falling*
> *And even the occasional visitor*
> *Has ceased to come*
> *Along the precipitous path of the Yoshino Peaks.*

Hopes Dashed

In January that next year, Father was looking forward with happy expectation to the night when he might be appointed as governor of a province. In this, he was disappointed, and the next morning we received a letter from someone who had equally been disappointed, saying:

I anxiously waited for the dawn with uncertain hope that this time around we might be appointed.

The temple bell roused me from dreams
And waiting for the starlit dawn
The night, alas! was long as are
One hundred autumn nights.

I wrote back:

> *Long was the night.*
> *The bell called from dreams in vain,*
> *For it did not toll*
> *The fulfillment of our hopes.*

Higashiyama

Toward the end of April, we moved to a house near Higashiyama.[31] On the way there, I saw the nursery beds along the roadside, some of them filled with water, and others already planted with young rice plants, so that they were covered in a splendid green hue. But the nearby mountains threw a dark shadow over the house and I felt lost when in the silent dark the water rails began to chatter:

> *The water rails cackle*
> *As if they were knocking at the gate,*
> *But who would be deceived*
> *Into opening the door, saying,*

Our friend has come along the mountain path
In the dark night?

Our house was near the Ryōsen temple and I went there to worship.[32] As it was a steep climb, we stopped at a well in the mountain, and when we scooped up water with our hands to drink from it, one of my companions said, "I could never have enough of this water."

I said:

> *Now you've slaked your thirst*
> *With this mountain water*
> *From the hollow of your hand*
> *Yet you've still not had your fill.*

She replied,

> *It is sweeter than to drink*
> *From a shallow spring,*
> *Muddy from the drops that fall*
> *From the hand that scoops it.*

On our return home the bright setting sun lit up the town below us.

My friend, who had exchanged poems with me said she had to return to the capital. I was sorry to part with her and sent word the next morning:

> *Gazing at the evening sun*
> *As she descends behind the mountain peak,*
> *I think with longing*
> *Of you at Higashiyama.*

From the house, we could hear the precious sound of priests reciting *sūtra* at their morning service. When I opened the shutters, I could faintly see the morning mist draped in veils across the mountain ridge's dim treetops.

Unlike the splendor of blossoms or red leaves, there was a special grace in the scenery, in the way in which the crowded treetops punctuated the dim and clouded sky while a *hototogisu* sang out on a nearby branch:

> *O for a friend—*
> *That we might see*

And listen together!
O the beautiful dawn
In the mountain village!—
The call of hototogisu
Near and far away.

On this last day in April, there was a chorus of *hototogisu* singing clamorously from treetops throughout the Valley:

Those who dwell in the capital
May long to hear the hototogisu *sing*
Yet here you are
Singing from dusk till dawn.

Thus we were languishing together and gazing at the surrounding scenery when a court lady who was with me said, "Do you think someone in the capital might be listening to a *hototogisu* right now, and be thinking of us?"

Though many may gaze toward the moon,
Who will think of us
Deep among the mountains.

I replied:

> *Gazing at the moon,*
> *In the dead of night,*
> *None may know the mountains,*
> *Think though they might*
> *Of a place like this.*

Once, toward dawn, I heard something that sounded like the footsteps of a horde of people coming down the mountain. Getting up I looked out and saw a herd of deer that had drawn close to the veranda and were crying out. It was not pleasant to hear them from so close by:

> *It is best to hear the love call*
> *Of a deer to its mate,*
> *In autumn nights,*
> *Upon the distant hills.*

I heard that an acquaintance had been near to where we lived but had gone back without calling on me. So I wrote to her, saying:

Even this wandering wind
Among the pines of the mountain—
I've heard that it departs
With a murmuring sound.

On an early morning late in August, I was gazing at the dim and distant mountains and could hear the incomparably exquisite sound of a waterfall:

If only I could show
This lingering moon,
Over an autumn mountain village
To one who understands.

On our departure, I noticed how the rice paddies along the road, which had been all water on my arrival, had been harvested and were now lying bare.

The young plants in their bed of water—
The plants harvested—
The fields dried up—
So long I remained away from home.

When I briefly returned to Higashiyama toward the end of October, the leaves that had cast such a lush shade had all fallen and scattered. And even the stream that had coursed downhill so pleasantly had been buried, leaving only its course imprinted in the leaves.

> *Even the stream has gone*
> *Since I left from here*
> *Swept away like leaves upon the tempest*
> *Among these forlorn mountains.*

When I left again, I told a nun who lived at Higashiyama, "If I'm still alive come spring, I will surely return. So please let me know as soon as the flowers are in bloom again." But when, the next year, the tenth of March had passed, and she had still not sent word, I wrote to her, saying:

> *Did you fail your pledge*
> *To herald the flowers' peak*
> *Or has spring just failed us*
> *And robbed them of their color.*

Bamboo

We now moved to a house near a bamboo grove. At night, the wind rustled the bamboo leaves, causing me to lie awake, unable to close my eyes:

> *Night after night the bamboo leaves sigh,*
> *My dreams are broken and a vague,*
> *Indefinite sadness fills my heart.*

When we moved to yet another place in the autumn, I sent a letter to the house's owner:

> *I am like dew on the grass—*
> *Pitiable wherever I may be,*

But most of all I miss
Autumn's plain of cogon grass.

Name

My stepmother, who had taken her name from the province to which Father had been appointed was known by that name at court.[33] And when Father heard that she was still using that name, even though she had meanwhile married another man, he made me write to her on his behalf and let her know that this was no longer appropriate:

> *You, who now dwells among the clouds,*
> *Why do you still call yourself by your old name?*

Lady Ukifune

Living a life in idleness, I occasionally visited a temple, but even then I could never pray like others, with a pure heart. In those days people learned to recite *sūtra* and practice austerities of religious observance after the age of seventeen or eighteen, but I could scarcely even think of such matters.

All I could think and hope for was, *How lovely would it be if, only once a year, a high-class nobleman like the dashing Shining Prince Genji would come and visit me; and I would hide in some mountain village like a Lady Ukifune, spending her days gazing at the flowers, the turning leaves, the moon, and anxiously awaiting one of his splendid letters!*

I spent many years idly believing that, if only my parents were of high class, I too would be elevated in position, when at length Father was finally appointed governor to the distant province of Hitachi.

He said, "I was always hoping that if I could win a position as governor in the neighborhood of the capital I could take care of you to my heart's desire. I could then take you with me to see beautiful vistas of seas and mountains. Moreover, you could then live attended beyond the possibilities of our present position. But our *karma* from our previous lives must have been bad, so that I now have been appointed to such a distant and remote province. When I brought you down with me to Kazusa when you were still a little child, I was worried about what might happen to you if I should fall ill. How much more worrying is it to me to think how you would wander helplessly in that far country were I to die! When I just think of all the inconveniences of living in such a remote place, I myself might get along fine, but to think that I will have to bring along my whole family, without the freedom to speak and act as I please, simply breaks my heart. And now you are grown up I am not sure that I can live long. One often hears how girls fall into neglect in the capital after their parents die, yet how much more wretched would it be if you had to wander in the eastern province like any countrywoman. We have no blood relatives in the capital to take you in, yet neither can I refuse a governorship that has been granted after such long waiting. So you must remain here, and we must part forever. All I can pray for is that you will find a spouse who can provide for you in the capital."

Night and day he lamented, saying these things, and I grew so sad that I even lost the joy of looking at flowers or the turning leaves, and wondering what to do.

Farewell

Father went down on the thirteenth of July, but already five days before his departure, he stopped coming to my room as it became too painful to meet.

When the day of parting finally came and the house was in a state of commotion as the hour of parting approached,[34] I lifted the blinds of my room and my eyes met his, full of tears. I wanted to follow him out to see him off, but all went black and I collapsed on the floor.

One of the servants who would look after me in the capital, who had gone out him to see him off, returned with a scrap of paper with just a few lines:

If I could do as I wish

I could acknowledge more profoundly
The sorrow of departing in autumn.

My eyes filled with tears and I could not read the poem
to the end. I recalled how in happier times I had often tried
to compose broken-limbed poems, and so, feeling the urge
to write at least something, I replied:

Never did I think that I would be
Parted from you in this world,
Even for a moment.

Only few came to see me, and I fell into a state of lonely
and forlorn musing, trying to imagine where he might be.
As I knew the road to the east, I thought of him all the
more longingly and all the more disheartened, and spent
my days gazing at the ridges of the eastern mountains from
dawn till dusk.

To Uzumasa

In August I went to Uzumasa to spend some days at the temple.[35] Taking the Ichijō avenue, we came upon the carriages of two men who had stopped to wait for someone with whom they intended to visit the temple. When we passed by, they sent an attendant over with the message:

I see you're off to see the flowers!

I thought it would be unpolite not to reply to such an elegant letter, and answered:

Like so many flowers in the autumn fields
I may seem to you.

I stayed at the temple for seven days but could think of nothing but the road to the east.

I prayed to the Buddha, saying, "There is no way to change the present, but grant that we may meet again in good health." And I thought the Buddha would take pity on me and hear my prayer.

A Letter

Winter came and it was raining all day long. In the night a fierce wind blew away the clouds and the moon broke through to light up a clear night sky. I noticed how the silvergrass growing near the house was beaten down and broken by the wind and touched by the scene before me I wrote:

> *How they must long*
> *For the bounty of autumn*
> *The tempest lays them low*
> *In the depth of winter,*
> *Confused and broken.*

A messenger arrived from the east with a letter from Father:

On my rounds along the shrines of the province, I came upon a wide wooded field with a beautiful river running through it. My first thought was of you, and regretting I could not show it to you, I asked, "What is this place called?" And they answered, 'It is called Koshinobi—The Forest of Longing After One's Child." This struck a chord with me and made me very sad, and alighting from my horse, I stood there for many hours immersed in thought.

> *Oh, Forest of Koshinobi*
> *Have you too left behind your child?*
> *How sad to look on you!*

Needless to say that my heart ran over as I read his letter:

> *Hearing of Koshinobi Forest,*
> *I think with dread*
> *Of the eastern road,*
> *Beyond Mount Chichibu.*[36]

The Dream

Spending my days like this idleness I wondered why at least I did not go on a pilgrimage. But Mother, being extremely old-fashioned, said, "How dreadful; the Hase temple! What if we are kidnapped at Nararasaka? And the Ishiyama temple; then you have to cross the dreadful barrier at Sekiyama! And the Kurama temple; yet another mountain! It just terrifies me to think of taking you there! You had better wait until father returns…"

Thus troubling herself over me as if I were some neglected thing, Mother merely agreed to go for a stay at the nearby Kiyomizu temple. But as before, I could not shake off my old daydreaming habits and I could not fix my mind on prayer as I ought to.

In the equinoctial week, there was the great tumult of a festival, so great a noise that I was even afraid of it, and when I lay asleep I dreamt there was a priest within the enclosure before the altar, in blue garments with a loose brocade hood and brocade shoes. He seemed to be the intendant of the temple. "Unaware of the fate that awaits you, you are solely occupied with vain thoughts," he said indignantly and went behind the curtain. I awoke startled, but I did not tell what I had dreamt, nor did I give it any further thought.

The Mirror

Mother had a one-foot wide bronze mirror cast and, since she did not want to go there on a pilgrimage to the Hase temple with me, she entrusted it to a priest with the words, "Please go into retreat at the temple for three days and pray that my daughter may see her future in a dream." And during those three days, she made me also abstain from eating fish and meat.

When the priest returned he said, "I was reluctant to leave the temple without having seen a dream. Intent on returning with good tidings, I devoted myself with all my heart to my religious service, and when I eventually fell asleep, I dreamt a most chaste and noble-looking lady in beautiful garments appeared from behind the curtains. She took the suspended mirror down and said, 'Has the sender of this mirror attached a Buddhist prayer?' I respectfully said, 'There were no letters. I was merely told to offer this mirror.' 'That is strange!' she said. 'It should have come with a written Buddhist prayer. See what is mirrored here; how pitiful!' And saying this, she began to weep bitterly. I looked at the mirror and saw a figure rolling around on the floor, weeping and lamenting. 'Does it not make you sad to see this reflection?' she said. 'But watch this!' she continued as she turned the mirror. And now I saw a great number of fresh green blinds and from under the silk screen beyond the blinds, I saw a great abundance of many-layered and multi-colored garments spilling forth; while in the garden outside, the plum and cherry trees were in bloom and an *uguisu* was singing and flitting among the branches. 'Now this makes one happy,' she said. And this was the content of my dream."

At the time, I did not show any interest in how these dreams might foretell my future, and I did not really listen to what the monk had to say. Unfaithful person that I was, people repeatedly said to me, "You should offer prayers to Amaterasu Ōmikami." But I merely thought, *Where is this god?* Or *Might it be Buddha himself?* But gradually I gained more insight and when I asked people about it, they said, "She is a goddess, and takes up her abode at Ise. The goddess is also worshipped by the provincial governor of Kii. She is also worshipped as the guardian deity at the Imperial Court's ancestor shrine."

I could hardly think of going all the way to Ise, nor could I go and worship at the court's ancestral shrine, so how could I pay homage to this god? The idea passed through my mind to pray to the heavenly light.

Winter

A relative of mine became a nun and entered the Sugaku temple. In winter I sent her a poem:

> *Even tears arise for your sake*
> *When I think of the mountain hamlet*
> *Where snowstorms rage.*

She replied:

> *I seem to have a glimpse of you*
> *Coming to me through a dark wood,*
> *When close overhead*
> *Is summer's growth of leaves.*

Bird Clappers

Father, who had gone down toward the east, came back at last. He settled down at Nishiyama, and we all went there. We were very happy. One moonlit night we talked all night through:

> *Such nights as this exist!*
> *As if it were for eternity, I parted from you—*
> *How sad was that autumn!*

At this, father shed tears of happiness abundantly, and answered me with a poem:

> *That life grows dear*

And is lived with rejoicing
Which once was borne
With hate and lamentation.

My joy knew no bounds when my waiting was at an end after I had believed we had parted forever. Father said: "It is ridiculous to lead a worldly life when one is very old. I used to feel so when I saw old men, but now I have grown old myself, so I will retire from social life." He said it with no lingering affection for this world, and I felt quite alone.

Toward the east, the fields stretched far and wide and I could see clearly from Mount Hiei to Mount Inari. Toward the west, I could hear the wind in the pines of the forest of Narabigaoka, and up to the plateau on which our house stood, the rice fields were cultivated in terraces, while from them came the sound of the bird-scaring clappers, which lent the place a rural atmosphere.

On moonlit evenings I often stayed up late to take in the scenery. As we lived far away from the capital, we had only few visitors, but one day I received a message from an old acquaintance who had an opportunity to write to me, and I wrote back:

None calls upon me,
Or remembers me in my mountain village.
Through the reeds by the thin hedge,
Autumn winds are sighing.

To Court

In October we moved back again to the capital. Mother had become a nun, and although she lived in the same house, shut herself up in a separate chamber. Father rather treated me as an independent woman than as his child. I felt helpless to see him shunning all society and living hidden in the shade.

Princess Yuko, the daughter of the Emperor Toshiyaku, who had heard about me through a distant relative, called me to her, saying it would be better for me to be with her than to spend my days in idleness.

My old-fashioned parents thought that court life would be very unpleasant, and wanted me to spend my time at home, but others said, "People nowadays go out as ladies-in-waiting at court, where fortunate opportunities for marriage are naturally numerous; why not try it?" So at the age of twenty-six Father reluctantly sent me to court.

I went for just one night the first time. I was dressed in an eight-fold *uchigi* of deep and pale chrysanthemum colors, and over it, I wore an outer robe of deep-red silk.

My mind having been totally absorbed in romances, except for those from whom I had borrowed books, I knew no one from whom I could learn distinguished manners or court customs. I had always been in the shadow of my old-fashioned parents, and had been accustomed to stay in and gaze at the moon and the flowers. So when I left home, I felt out of my depth, estranged from the world, and I returned home in the early morning.

I had often fancied in my countrified mind that I should hear more interesting things for my heart's consolation than were to be found living at home in my parents' house. But at court, I felt awkward in everything I did, and I thought it sad, But what could I do?

Filial Piety

In December I went to court again. A room was assigned for my use and I stayed for several days.

Every night, I was summoned to the princess's apartment and had to lay down among unknown persons, so I could not sleep at all. I was bashful and timid and wept in secret. In the morning I retired to my room while it was still dark and passed the days in longing for home where my old and weak parents, making much of me, relied upon me as if I were worthy of it. And I grieved over my nieces, who had lost their mother and had been cared for by me alone, even sleeping at night one on either side of me.

Spending my days in vacant musing, I felt as if someone were constantly spying upon me, and I was embarrassed.[37]

When I was allowed to return home after some ten days, Father and mother were waiting for me with a comfortable fire in a brazier.

Seeing me getting out of my carriage, Father said, "When you were with us people came to see us, but now no one's voice is heard, no one can be seen among the house. We feel sad and lonely. What will happen to us if you stay at court?" It was pitiful to see them cry when he said it.

The next morning they sat before me, saying: "Now you are here, many persons are coming and going and the house seems alive again." Tears came to my eyes to think what virtue I could have that my parents made so much of me.

It would be very difficult even for a saint to dream of his previous life. Yet, when I was before the altar of the Kiyo-mizu temple, in a faintly dreamy state of mind, neither sleeping nor waking, I saw a man who seemed to be the head of the temple. He came out and said to me:

"You were once a priest of this temple and you were born into a better state by virtue of the many Buddhist images you carved as a Buddhist artist. The seventeen-foot-high Buddha that is enthroned in the eastern wing of the temple was your work. When you were in the act of covering it with gold foil you died."

"Oh, undeservedly blessed!" I said. "I will finish it, then."

The priest replied: "As you died, another man covered it with gold and performed votive offerings."

If only I had acted on this dream and paid worship at the Kiyomizu temple—the very place where I had worshipped in my previous life. But as usual, I did not trouble myself to make any further pilgrimages to the temple.

Dropwort

On the twenty-fifth of December, I was summoned by the princess to the religious service of reciting Buddha's names. I went for that night only. About forty ladies were there, all dressed in white under-robes covered with deep-red outer robes. I sat behind the person who had introduced me at court—the most shadow-like person among them.

I retired before dawn, and on my way home it snowed in fluttering flakes, and the frozen, ghostly moon was reflected in my dull-red sleeves of glossy silk, so that it seemed as if even the moon were shedding tears:

> *The year draws to a close*
> *And even while*

The moon shines faintly on my sleeve
So does the night give way today.

I had long thought, *When at court, I might become familiar with those who serve there, and know its workings better, and if they come to like me, they might receive me as a lady and favor me.* But for some reason, Father grew disappointed in me and told me to come home. Yet how could I have expected my fortunes to improve overnight? It had rather been an idle fancy:

> *Though a thousand times, how many!*
> *I gathered dropwort in the fields*
> *Yet my wishes remained unanswered.*[38]

These thoughts were graven in my mind.

At Court

My life now grew very busy. I forgot about my books and became more earnest, and I wondered how I had idly wasted all those years, without observing my religious practices or going on pilgrimages. I even began to doubt whether any of my romantic notions were even real. Could someone like the Shining Prince Genji really have lived in this world? This was not a world in which General Kaoru kept his lover hidden in Uji. What on earth had I been thinking? What shallowness!

But if I believed I could turn my life around, I was sorely mistaken. No one at court really believed I had gone home after my initial stint, and I was constantly summoned and even told, "Bring along your young nieces!"

And thus I was forced to bring along my nieces, on top of which I had to also attend myself. As the days fled by, I gradually lost my vain hopes. Even on those occasions when my nieces dragged me along to be in attendance, those who *were* familiar with court life went around with such airs that I—neither an inexperienced youth nor a senior court lady—was left in the uncomfortable position of being discarded as just an occasional visitor. Yet since I did not want to wait on the princess in earnest, I felt no envy toward those who were treated with more respect than me. I rather felt it as a relief, and only attend at suitable occasions, when I could while away the hours by chatting with those around me. And even on special occasions or festivities, I refrained from mingling with the others, or stand out and be noticed. Instead, I would just spend my time listening to what was being generally said.

On one very bright moonlit night in April, I attended the princess to the imperial palace. I remembered that I wanted to use such an occasion to pay homage to Amaterasu Ōmikami, who was enthroned within the court's shrine. And, that month, on a moonlit night, I stole myself there to meet up with Lady Hakase. By the faint light of the candles, she looked wondrously old and holy. She seemed unlike a mortal—a divine incarnation, and spoke very gracefully.

The moon was very bright on the following night, when I and some of the princess's ladies-in-waiting were passing the time in talking and moon-gazing from the opened outer shutters of the Fujitsubo Pavilion.[39] We heard the footsteps of the Umetsubo consort going up to the emperor's pavilion—they were so exquisitely graceful as to excite envy. "Had the late empress been still alive, she could not walk so grandly," someone said, which moved me so, that I composed a poem:

> *She is like the moon, who,*
> *Opening the gates of heaven,*
> *Ascends above the clouds.*
> *We, being in the same heavenly palace,*
> *Pass the night*
> *Remembering the footfalls of the past.*

One winter night, when the moonless and cloudless sky was lit up by bright stars, I and the ladies in attendance on the chancellor passed the hours talking idly. Afterward, one of the ladies, who had left the court, remembered that night and wrote to me:

> *That moonless,*
> *flowerless winter night*
> *It penetrates my thought*
> *And makes me dwell on it—*
> *I wonder why?*

It touched my heart that she should have remembered that night, and I replied:

> *In my dreams*
> *The tears of that cold night*
> *Are still frozen.*
> *But these I weep away in secret.*

One night, while I was sleeping near the princess, I was awakened by a sound of fluttering water jowls in the pavilion's pond:

Like us the water jowl
Pass the night in floating sleep,
Weary with shaking off
Their feathers' frost.

The lady-in-waiting who was lying next to me heard this and replied:

How much more pitied, then, am I—
I, who must languish like the water jowl
Shake off the frost from my sleeves.

One day, a lady-in-waiting with whom I was close, opened the sliding doors that separated our rooms, and we passed our leisure time talking about romances. We repeatedly invited a mutual friend, who was waiting on the princess, to come and join us, and she replied. "I will come over if it is important." To which I replied:

The long leaves of the reed are easily bent,
So I will not lean on it,
But leave it to the wind.

An Encounter

The ladies-in-waiting charged with introducing court nobles had fixed positions, so that inexperienced outsiders like me did not stand a chance of being chosen—indeed, I wasn't even noticed.

But one very dark night early in October, when sweet-voiced priests were reciting *sūtra* throughout the night, I and another lady-in-waiting went out toward the entrance door of the audience room to listen. We lay there listening and chatting when I noticed a gentleman had come for an audience with the princess.

My companion said, "It is awkward to run away to our rooms. But that would be unbecoming. We will remain here!" So and I sat there, listening to their conversation.

He spoke gently and quietly. "Who is the other lady?" he asked of my friend, but there was nothing rude or amorous in his voice like other men. Instead, he talked delicately of the sad, sweet things of this world, and many a phrase of his had a strange power that drew me into their conversation, in spite of myself. He was surprised to find someone at court who was still a stranger to him, and he did not seem inclined to leave anytime soon.

There was no starlight, and a gentle shower fell in the darkness; how lovely was its sound on the leaves! "What a remarkable night, is it not?" he said. "A moonlit night would be too dazzling, too vulgar."

He went on to talk about the beauties of spring and autumn, saying, "Although every season has its charm, how charming is the spring haze. Then the sky being tranquil and overcast, the face of the moon is not too bright but seems to be floating on a distant river. At such a time a calm spring melody on the *biwa* is exquisite.

"In autumn, on the other hand, the moon is very bright, and, though there are mists trailing over the horizon, we can see things as clearly as if they were close at hand. The breath of the wind, the voice of insects, all seem to blend

together. When at such a time we listen to the autumnal music of the *koto* we forget all about spring.

"But then, when I think of winter nights, the sky frozen all over in a magnificent frost, he snow covering the earth and reflecting the moonlight! Then the notes of the *hitchiriki* vibrate on the lucid air and we forget all about spring and autumn."

Then he asked us, "Which captivates your heart? On which stays your mind?"

My companion said it was autumn nights but I, not willing to imitate her, said:

> *Pale green night and flowers*
> *All melt into one*
> *In the soft haze—*
> *Everywhere the moon,*
> *Glimmering in the spring night.*

And he, tasting my lines on his lips, said: "Then you give up autumn? And he continued:

> *After this, as long as I live,*

Each spring night
Shall be for me a memento of tonight.

My companion who favored autumn said:

Others seem to give their hearts to spring,
And I shall be alone gazing at the autumn moon,

He was fascinated by our answers and said, "Even Chinese poets could not decide which to praise most, spring or autumn. Your choices make me think that there must be some special reason why our inclination is touched or charmed. Our souls are imbued with the colors of the sky, moon, or flowers of that moment. I wonder what made you chose one or the other. The moon on a winter night has long been given as an instance of dreariness, and as it is very cold I had never seen it intentionally.

"When I went down to Ise as the imperial envoy to attend the installation of the imperial princess at the shrine, I wanted to return at dawn, so I went to take leave of the princess in a moonlit night after many days of snow, dreading even the thought of being so far away from home.

"Her residence was this unbelievably other-worldly place, but she called me into a room fitting for the occasion. There were persons who had served at the shrine since the reign of Emperor Enyu. Their aspect was very holy, ancient, and mystical. They tearfully spoke of things that had long since passed and brought out a well-tuned *biwa*, and the music they played seemed out of this world.

I regretted that day should dawn, and was touched so deeply that I had almost forgotten about returning to the capital. Ever since then the snowy nights of winter recall that scene, and without fail I gaze at the moon even while I hug the fire. You will surely understand me, and my heart too will be touched by dark and rainy nights like this, for I feel it might well be equal to that snowy night at the palace of the imperial princess at the Ise shrine."

With these words, he departed and I realized he still did not know who I was.

In August next year, we went again to the imperial palace, where a concert was held that lasted throughout the night. I did not know that he was in attendance, and I passed the night in my room.

Early the next morning, I opened the sliding doors to the

corridor and looked out, and I saw the morning moon very faint and beautiful. I heard footsteps and people approaching, one of them reciting a *sūtra*. He stopped in front of my room and addressed me. I replied, and he, suddenly remembering, exclaimed, "That night of softly falling rain. How could I forget? Even for a moment! I yearn for it." As there was only little time, I said:

> *How could a gentle shower,*
> *Falling on leaves*
> *Remain so vivid in your mind?*

I had scarcely said so when people came up and I stole back without his answer.

That evening, after I had gone to my room, my companion came in to tell me that he had replied to my poem:

> *If there be such a tranquil night*
> *As that of the rain,*
> *I should like to make you listen to my lute,*
> *Playing all the songs I can remember.*

I wanted to hear it and waited for the fit occasion, but it never came.

That spring, one a tranquil evening, I heard he had again come to the princess's pavilion, so I crept out of my room with my companion, but there were many people waiting within and without the pavilion, and I stole back into my room. He must have been of the same mind as I; he had come because it was so still a night, but had returned because it was so noisy:

> *I yearn for a tranquil moment*
> *To be out upon the sea of harmony,*
> *In that enchanted boat.*
> *Oh, boatman, do you know my heart?*

And that was the end of it. He was a man of exceptional character— not easily encountered in this world. But time passed, and neither of us inquired after the other.

To Seki

I now deeply regretted the idle fancies of my old days, and as my parents would not accompany me to temples on pilgrimages I could hardly suppress my impatience. I wished to strengthen my spirit, and to raise my child, who was still just a budding sprout, I wanted to save up a storehouse full of virtuous deeds for the life to come. And thus, taking courage, I went to the Ishiyama temple toward the end of November.

It snowed and the route was lovely. On coming in sight of the barrier at the Ōsaka Pass, I was reminded that it was also in winter when I passed it on my way up to Heian-kyō. Then also it was a windy and tempestuous day. So I wrote:

The sound of the autumn wind
At the barrier of Ōsaka!
It differs not
From that heard long ago.

The temple at Seki, magnificent though it was, made me think of the old, roughly hewn Buddha. The beach at Uchide had not changed with the passing of years.

Toward evening I arrived at the temple and after a bath went up to the main shrine. I could not hear a voice, but terrified by the mountain wind, I dozed off during religious service, I had a dream in which someone said to me, "From the inner shrine perfume has been bestowed on us. Tell it at once." Startled, I awoke, and I realized it was just a dream, but thinking it might be auspicious, I passed the night in prayer.

The next day the wind raged and it snowed heavily. I comforted my lonely heart with someone whom I had befriended at court and who had come with me. We left the temple after three days.

Pilgrimage

On the twenty-fifth of October of the next year, the capital was in a state of great excitement over the purification ceremonies of the Daijō festival.[40] And it was on that same day that I wanted to set out for the Hase temple for my own religious purification. People around me said, "This is something you can see only once in a reign! Even the country people come to see the procession!" My brother angrily said, "It is madness to leave the city on this very day! You will become a running rumor!"

But the father of my baby children said, "No, no, let her do as she pleases," and according to my wish he let me start. His kindness touched me, but at the same time, I pitied those in my retinue who accompanied me, who longed to see the ceremony. But I thought, *What have I to do with such shows? Buddha will be pleased with those who come at a time like this.*

I wanted without fail to receive the divine favor and started before dawn. I was crossing the great bridge of Nijō, accompanied by attendants in white robes, who were running ahead carrying pine torches, when a great crowd on horseback, in carriages, and on foot, who were coming toward us on their way to the stands prepared for sightseers, called out in surprise, "What is that? What is that?" And there were even those who laughed or scolded me.

When we passed the house of the commander of the palace guard at Yoshinori, we found the gate wide open toward the galleries. The guards laughed and said, "Here goes a company to the temple—what a day to pick!" But one of them, who seemed kind, said seriously: "What is it to feast the eyes for just a moment? This person is firmly determined. She will surely see Buddha's compassion. This is no good. We should quit the sightseeing and do the same.

I had started out in the middle of the night to avoid the crowd, and to wait for those who had left later, as well as for the thick fog to lift, we made a stop at the great gate of the Hōsō temple. Those who had come up from the country to see the spectacle formed a veritable river. Nobody could turn aside to make room for anybody else, and even the ill-behaved and vulgar children, who pushed past my carriage, were startled at the sight.

I began to regret I had started out that day, yet praying to Buddha with all my heart, I arrived at the ferry of Uji. But even there the people were coming up to the city in throngs, and the ferrymen, seeing the countless people who were waiting to be put over, assumed an air of importance. Raising their sleeves, they just stood there in their boats, leaning against their poles, whistling and looking around indifferently, and refusing to bring their boats up along the riverbank.

We had to wait for a long time, so I had a good look at the place. Since Lady Murasaki's tale mentions how the daughter of the princess of Uji lived here, I was curious to see what it was like, and I found it a charming place.

I was still mesmerized by the place, when we finally managed to cross the river. When I saw the mansion of the general of Uji, I was at once reminded that the Lady Ukifune of the romance had been living here.

As we had started before daybreak, my people were tired out, and we stopped for a rest at Yahiroichi. While we were eating, one of the guards said: "Is that not the notorious Mount Kurikoma? It is growing dark. Do not lose sight of your armor and personal effects!" I listened to these words with a shudder, but we passed the mountain without mishap and arrived by the side of the Nieno Pond as the sun was just setting over the mountains. My men now went in several directions saying, "Let's find a place to stay!" But they returned saying, "There is no suitable place, except for an obscure hovel." So I said, "It can't be helped," and decided to stay there for the night.

The house had only two vulgar manservants, the rest having all gone up to the capital. They did not sleep at all that night but kept pacing up and down the house. One of my maids asked, "Why are you walking about like this?" And thinking that I was fast asleep, they said, "Listen; we have rented our house to perfect strangers. What should we do if our kettles were stolen? Of course we cannot sleep!" I was both disgusted and amused at the same time.

I set off in the early morning and went to the Tōdai temple to worship. The Isonokami shrine, too, looked truly ancient and I was almost sad to see how very much it had fallen into ruin.

That night we lodged at a temple in a place called Yamanobe. I was utterly exhausted and in pain, and fell asleep reading part of the lotus *sūtra*, when, in my dream, I saw a beautifully pure and noble woman. But when I went up to her, a fierce wind began to blow. When she noticed me, she smiled and said, "For what purpose have you come?"

I answered, "How could I help coming?"

"You should go back to the imperial palace," she said, "and you should have a good talk with Lady Hakase!" And I was delighted and encouraged.

We crossed the Hase River and arrived at the temple at nightfall. Having taken ablutions, I went up to the main hall. I remained at the temple for three days, and fell asleep the third night expecting to start out early in the morning, when I dreamt that a monk came down from the main hall and threw something into the room saying, "This is a holy cedar twig bestowed by the god Inari.[41] I awoke startled, when I realized it was just a dream.

We began our return journey before dawn and, as we could not find a place to stay, we took lodgings after we

had crossed the Nara Slope. And this too was a very small house. Someone said, "This is a strange place. Do not close an eye! And don't be frightened, as something unexpected may happen! Just lie down quietly and pretend you are asleep." And I spent the night feeling miserable and afraid, and it felt the night lasted for a thousand years.

When morning finally came, someone said, "This is a robber's den; the mistress of the house is up to no good."

We crossed the Uji River in a storm and the ferry passed very close to the wickerwork fish traps along the side of the river:

Today, indeed,
I can count the ripples
Around the wickerwork fish traps.

Writing down these events randomly, two, three, four, or five years after they have happened, my life seems to be that of one long pilgrimage, but it is not so. I am recording the events of several years.

Kurama

In the spring I went to go into seclusion at the Kurama temple. It was a soft spring day, with mist trailing over the mountain slopes. The mountain people brought *tokoro* root they had dug up and which was very tasteful. Along the mountain road on our way back, all the flowers had fallen and withered and there was nothing much to see.

When I went back in October, the mountain views along the way were more beautiful than before, the mountainside brocaded with the autumn colors. The sprays of water thrown up by the rushing mountain streams landed on the slopes in scattered crystals and wherever I looked the vistas were equally breathtaking.

I reached the monastery and entered the monk's quarters

when I noticed the maple leaves, glistening with the moist
of a soft drizzle—it was simply breathtaking:

> *The pattern of the maple leaves*
> *Dyed by autumnal rain—*
> *Beautiful beyond compare!*

Under a Clear Sky

After some two years, I again went into seclusion at Ishiyama. This time it was raining heavily all night long. I heard someone say how troublesome it was to travel with rain when, raising one of the latticed shutters, I looked out and it was so clear that I could see all the way to the bottom of the valley, which was bathing in the bright moonlight. And what I thought was rain, was a stream rippling among the roots of the trees.

The sound of the mountain brook
Gives an illusion of raindrops,
Yet the calmly waning moon
Covers all.

I again visited the Hase temple, my journey was not so solitary as before. Along the route, various persons invited us in, and we made but slow progress. The autumn leaves at the Hahaso forest in Yamashiro were beautiful. We crossed the Hase River, and I took heart from a poem I composed:

> *Like the turning Hase River,*
> *I have returned,*
> *Hoping to see the miracle*
> *Of the cedar twig.*

When we returned after three days, there were too many of us to lodge in the small house on the other side of the Nara Pass, so we camped in the field. Our men passed the night lying on *mukabaki* spread on the grass and covered with straw mats and spend a short night in which they slept little, their heads wet with dew. The dawn moon was perfectly clear and other-worldly:

> *Even in our wandering journey,*
> *The lonely moon accompanies us*

The waning moon I used to gaze at
Back in the capital.

As I could do as I liked, I went even to distant temples for worship, and my heart was consoled by the delights and hardships on the way, assured that they would bring me divine favor. Untrammeled by personal sorrows, I sought to raise my young children in the manner I thought best and waited impatiently for the passing of time. And I found solace in the sustained hope that the man upon whom I depended might find himself a decent appointment.

A Friend

I had one dear friend with whom I used to talk a lot, and with whom I would spend day and night exchanging poems. And though perhaps not as often as before, she kept sending me letters, until she married the governor of Echizen and went down to that province. After that, all communication between us ceased, so I wrote her a poem finding the means of sending it to her with great difficulty:

Undying affection!
Can it end at last,
Overlaid with time
Even as snow covers the land
In the northern province?

She wrote back:

Even a little pebble does not cease to be,
Though pressed under the snow of Mount Haku;
So is my hidden affection.

More Pilgrimages

Early in March, I went down among the hills of
Nishiyama. Not a person was to be seen and the whole
place was cloaked in silence and shrouded in mist. Only the
flowers bloomed in profusion, elegant and almost forlorn:

> *Far from the crowds,*
> *Along a mountain road,*
> *The cherry blooms and withers*
> *For none to see.*

One time, when our marriage was troubled, I went for a
retreat to Uzuma when I received a message from a senior
court lady who had often spoken to me and listened to

what I had to say. While I was passing my reply on to the messenger, I could hear the temple bell and penned down a poem for her:

> *The outer world of many sorrows*
> *Is not to be forgotten even here.*
> *At the sound of the evening bell*
> *My heart grows lonely.*

Palace Garden

One day, I was talking to two like-minded friends at the beautiful and tranquil palace of the princess. The next day, having returned home without much to do, I thought longingly of them and wrote to them:

> *Knowing the place of our meeting*
> *To be a windswept coast,*
> *Where memories ripple,*
> *and affections flow back,*
> *Yet I think with fondness*
> *Of you, who ventured with me.*

One of them wrote back:

To that windswept coast,
So we ventured,
But came up empty-handed
But for our wetted sleeves!

And the other:

Who would venture into the sea of tears
Seeking for a chance with zealous care,
Had not the flowers of lovely vision floated in it!

Waking

I had another dear friend who was of the same mind as me and with whom I likewise talked about the joys and hardships of this world, who went down to the province of Chikuzen.

Afterward, during a very bright, moonlit night, I fell asleep thinking with fondness of the times we had met at the palace, gazing at the moon and staying up all night. I then dreamed I went up to the palace and that we met each other, just as if it was really happening. I awoke startled, realizing it was just a dream. By now the moon had sunk where it hung just above the ridges of the Nishiyama hills, and I thought of the old song *I Did Not Want to Wake*, and I grew all the more pensive:

Tell her, oh, westbound moon,
That dreaming of her I could sleep no more,
But all the night
My pillow was bedewed with loving tears.

Ishizu

That autumn, I went down to the province of Izumi. From Yodo onward, the splendid journey downriver aroused emotions in me that are hard to put into words.

We spent the night at Takahama. It was dark, and in the depths of the night I heard the sound of an oar, and when someone asked, it turned out that women of pleasure were coming our way. My companions grew excited and called their boat to come alongside ours. In the flickering light of distant fires their long, tapering sleeves lit up as they opened their fans, shaded their faces, and sang—the scene was simply breathtaking.

The next evening, when the sun was just about to sink behind the crest of the mountains, we passed the inlet of

Sumiyoshi. The mist hung over all, blending the sky and the whole scenery—the treetops of the pines, the surface of the sea, the waves into one to create an image that cannot be captured in a painting, no matter how accomplished the hand of the artist:

> *What can I say?*
> *To what can I compare it?*
> *That splendid autumn evening*
> *At Sumiyoshi.*

I took in this scene as we passed by in our boat, wanting to take it in, again and again, unable to get enough.

In the winter I wanted to return to the capital and embarked by boat from Ōtsu Bay. But that night a tempest raged with such fury that the very rocks seemed to shake. The peels of thunder overhead, the beating waves, the howling winds, made me feel as if I were going to die.

They dragged the boat ashore, where we spent the night. Though the rain stopped, the gale continued to rage, and they could not put the boat out to sea. Unable to do

anything about it, we had to spend five or six days on the beach.

When the winds finally began to wane, I rolled up the boat's bamboo screen and looked out. The evening tide was rising swiftly and cranes called to each other in the bay.

Local officials came to see us, and said things like, "If you had left the bay last night to try and make it to Ishizu, your boat would have gone under without a trace." And I listened to them in terror:

> *Off Ishizu, in the wild sea*
> *The boat, driven before the storm*
> *Fades away and is seen no more.*
> *The wild gusts drive the boat—*
> *Into the wild sea she disappears—*
> *Off Ishizu!*

Parting

I devoted myself to my worldly duties, and if they had only let me, my service at court, too, might have turned out well, but since I only attended every now and then, it never amounted to much. As I began to put on years, I felt it unbecoming to behave as young couples do. In the meantime, my health declined and I could no longer go on as many pilgrimages as I wanted. My occasional stints in attendance grew less and less, and I began to believe that I had not much longer to live and I spent every waking and sleeping hour fretting how I could somehow see the future of my children secured while I was still alive.

We were anxiously waiting for my husband to be appointed. The announcement came that autumn, but it was not to the kind of province we had hoped. It was truly unsatisfactory and regrettable.

It was not so distant as the long road to the east I had traveled on Father's return, so I accepted the inevitable, and we hastily made preparations for his pending departure. We decided to start out around the tenth of October, and from the house where his daughter had recently moved.[42] Unaware of what was to come, the days leading up to his departure were busy with people gathered in high spirits.

When he finally went down on the 27th, our son went with him. He wore an autumn cloak over a glossy scarlet undergarment and aster-colored trousers,[43] and suspended from his waist a longsword. He came out behind my husband, who was wearing pale indigo trousers and a patterned overcoat, and they mounted their horses at the veranda.

When they had departed in a clamor, I felt utterly at a loss, though I was less disheartened when I was told that the province was not that distant.

The people who accompanied them to see them off returned the next day and said things like, "It has been an impressive departure!" And when someone said "This morning, I saw the spirit of a dead person come flying toward the capital,"[44] I believed it to be one of the men who had set out with my husband. How could I have realized that it was an omen of what was to come?

Death

While my husband and son were away I spent my time looking after my children and was merely concerned with raising them to be good adults. But in April, the next year, my husband returned and spent the summer and autumn at home. Then, on the 25th of September, he fell ill. And when, on the 5th of October, he passed away, all became like a dream, and the depth of my grief was unlike anything I had experienced before. And I realized that the image of the rolling figure on the floor the monk had seen in the mirror my mother had offered to the Hase temple was a glimpse of my present condition. The auspicious image on the mirror's reverse side had not come to pass, nor would it ever be realized in the future.

On the night of the 23rd, we cremated my husband and the remains of his fleeting existence on earth were reduced to smoke. Our son, who had gone down with him the previous autumn, being dressed exquisitely and much attended, was dressed in a ghastly white mourning tunic over black clothes as he followed the cart with his father's coffin and wept. My feelings when I saw him going out can never be expressed. I seemed to live in a dream and wondered if my deceased husband would be able to see me like this.

If only I had given my heart over to those endless tales and poems and dedicated myself day and night to earnest devotion, this dreadful nightmare would never have become reality. If, on my first visit to the Hase temple, when I dreamt of the priest who said, "This is a holy cedar twig bestowed by the god Inari!"—if I had only then immediately set out on a pilgrimage to the Inari shrine, all this would never have happened. All these years I had believed that my recurring dream in which I was told to "Pray to Amaterasu Ōmikami" meant that I was destined to become a high-ranking wetnurse who served at the imperial palace and was favored by the emperor and empress. But none of it had come true, except for the pitiful figure in the mirror. In this frame of mind, as someone whose wishes had failed to materialize, I drifted through life, unable to perform a single pious act.

Amida Buddha

Thus my life dragged on amid hardships and I even began to worry whether my wishes for my afterlife might be granted. I had just one piece of solace. On the night of the 13th of October, in the year of Tenki, I dreamt that Amida Buddha was standing in the garden of the house where I was living. I could not see his distinct figure, but only faintly, as if through a veil of mist. Straining my eyes, I could see him through a lifted shroud, standing on a three- or four-foot-high lotus flower pedestal. He was about six feet high and bathed in a golden light. One of his hands was stretched out to me; the fingers of the other bent in benediction. None but I could see him, yet I felt such reverence that I dared not approach the blinds to see him more

up close. Then he said, "Well then, I will leave now, but I will come for you later." And only I could hear him speak, the others apparently unable to hear. When I woke up with a start, the next day had already dawned.

From then onward, this dream was my sole consolation.

Obasute

I lived in our old house with my nephews and saw them every day. But after these sad events, they all went their separate ways and I hardly saw anyone anymore.

One dark night, the youngest of them came to see me, and puzzled, I said:

> *No moon, and darkness deepens*
> *Around Oba-sute.*[45]
> *Why have you come?*
> *It cannot be to see the moon!*

After that, an intimate friend stopped writing altogether, and I wrote to her:

You may think I have left this world,
Yet here I am
Weeping my days away.

In October, on a brightly moonlit night, I gazed at the moon and wept and wept:

Though my heart is clouded by tears
Still I gaze
At the bright moon.

Mugwort

Years and months have since fled by. But even now, when I recall that bad dream in which I lost my husband, my heart is thrown into turmoil and everything before my eyes seems to go black, so that I cannot bring myself to think clearly of that time.

Now, everyone has moved away to live elsewhere, and I remain alone in my old home, helpless and forlorn.

One bad night, when I could not sleep, I wrote a poem to someone from whom I had not heard in a long time:

> *Wild the mugwort grows*
> *And moist with dew*
> *Alike my sleeves with tears,*

No sound of visitors
Just my sobbing.

She had become a nun and replied:

Mugwort is found at worldly dwellings
But spare a thought for those
Who must seek their gardens
Among the weeds.

Glossary

<table>
<tr><td>aoi:</td><td>Also futaba-aoi: At the great festival of the Kamo shrine in Heian-kyō the participants crowned their heads with the leaves of this plant, so it must have been well known.</td></tr>
<tr><td>biwa:</td><td>A four- or five-stringed lute played with a large-sized plectrum.</td></tr>
<tr><td>dera or tera:</td><td>Temple.</td></tr>
<tr><td>hakama:</td><td>Trousered skirt.</td></tr>
<tr><td>hichiriki:</td><td>Pipe made of seven reeds having a very clear, piercing sound.</td></tr>
<tr><td>hototogisu:</td><td>Lesser cuckoo (Cuculus poliocephalus), a bird native to Japan.</td></tr>
</table>

karakasa: Large paper umbrella.

kichō: Kind of screen used in upper-class houses.

koto: Thirteen-stringed musical instrument.

misu: Finer sort of *sudare* used in court or in Shintō shrine. It is made of thin finely woven bamboo curtain, behind which one may see but not be seen, used to screen off important personages, as well as women's apartments.

mukabaki: Kind of leather shield made of untanned deerskin worn hanging from the shoulder.

ogi no ha: Reed-leaf, a woman's name or pet name.

sudare: Older ladies avoided men's eyes and always sat behind *sudare* (finely split bamboo curtain) through which they could look out without being seen.

uguisu: Japanese bush warbler (*Horornis diphone*).

Notes

1:    Her father Sugawara no Takasue (b. 972) was ap-
      pointed Governor of Kazusa in 1017. The author,
      then nine years old, was brought from Kyoto to the
      Kazusa *kokufu*, the provincial capital (today's Ichihara
      city), where her father's mansion was situated.

2:    Prince Genji: The hero of the *Genji monogatari* by
      Murasaki Shikibu.

3:    Yakushi Buddha: The Buddha of healing; formally
      Bhaiṣajya-guru-vaiḍūrya-prabhā-rāja (Medicine Master
      and King of Lapis Lazuli Light).

4:    High personages, Governors of Provinces or other no-
      bles, traveled with a great retinue, consisting of armed

horsemen, foot-soldiers, and attendants of all sorts both high and low, together with the luggage necessary for a prolonged journey. In this case, the journey would have taken roughly three months.

5:   Chō, here, might indicate that Mano was a local chieftain or village headman.

6:   *Hama*, here, means beach (today's central Chiba city).

7:   Edo River. However, the border between the two provinces was not the Edo River, but the Sumida River.

8:   Having given birth to a baby, the wetnurse would have been considered "unclean."

9:   The Sumida River formed the border between Shimōsa and Musashi, not between Musashi and Sagami.

10:   Ariwara No Narihira (825–80) was a Heian courtier and poet whose amorous exploits are believed to be the subject of the *Ise monogatari*. In the passage referred to, Narihira, leaves a loved one behind when he crosses the Sumida River. While being ferried across the River, he catches sight of a white bird. Told by the ferryman it is called a *miyakodori*, or "bird of the capital." the poet exclaims:

If true to your name,
Then pray tell me, miyakodori:
Is the one I think of
Safe and sound?

11: The *Yamato nadeshiko* (*Dianthus superbus,* [subsp.] *long-icalycinus*), a delicately fringed pink flower. Its Japanese name combines the words Yamato, the ancient name for Japan, and *nadeshiko,* whose *kanji* translate into English as "caressable child."

12: According to *Sagami fūdoki,* this district was in ancient times inhabited by Koreans. The natives could not distinguish a Korean from a Chinese, hence the name of Morokoshigahara, or "Chinese Field." Hence the irony of the presence of the Yamato flower.

13 This seems to be the last line of a song called *imayo,* perhaps improvised by the singers. Naniwa-kyō (present-day Osaka) was the capital of Japan during the 7th and 8th century, before Nara, and then Kyoto.

14: In Japanese, *Futaba aoi* (*Asarum caulescens*), commonly known in the West as wild ginger. The plant is used in festivals of the Kamo shrine, so that it is also known as *Kamo aoi.* For the travelers, deep among the mountains, the plant must have reminded them of home.

15: Tago no Ura lay on the west bank of the Fuji River.

16: Yatsuhashi, or Eight Bridges, was a bridge made of eight long platforms crossing the iris marshes of Mikawa Province and is featured in the *Ise monogatari*, which is where the author must have read about it.

17: Shikasuga was a ford across the Toyo River. The lines to which the author is referring are from a poem by Lady Nakatsukasa (920–80):

Yukeba ari
Yukaneba kurushi
Shikasuga no
Watari ni kite zo
Omoiwazurau

Cross it or not
It will be painful
As expected,
Now I am about to cross
I am troubled.

18: The wide Seta River at the southern tip of Lake Biwa, was the last hurdle toward the capital.

19: Between 15:00 and 17:00. It was custom for well-to-do citizens of Heian-kyō to arrive well after dark when they had long been on the road, so that they would not be seen in their disheveled state.

20: Princess Shūshi (997–1049), the first daughter of Emperor Ichijō (986–1011).

21: One of her father's wives.

22: One of the three famous calligraphers of that time.

23: Place where people were cremated.

24: Books in those days were published chapter by chapter.

25: Situated just west of Kyoto, Uzumasa is the site of the ancient Kōryū temple, the oldest temple in Kyoto. It is said to have been built in 603 by Hata no Kawakatsu upon receiving a Buddhist statue from Prince Shōtoku Taishi.

26   In October it was the custom for all local gods to go for a conference to the residence of the oldest native god, in the province of Izumo.

27: The Rokkaku-dō, better known today as the Chōhō-*ji*,

is a Buddhist temple in Kyoto, and is believed to have been established by Prince Shōtoku. The name comes from its main hall's hexagonal (*rokkaku*) shape.

28: According to the superstition of those days people believed that every house was presided over by an earth god, which occupied the hearth in spring, the gate in summer, the well in autumn, and the garden in winter. It was dangerous to encounter this god when it changed abode.

29: The *Chang Hen Ge* (*Song of Everlasting Regret*) is a literary work from 809 by the famous Chinese poet Bai Juyi (772-846). It tells the love story of Tang Emperor Xuanzong and his favorite concubine Yang Guifei (719-756).

30: Titled *Kabane tazuneru miya* (*The Corpse-seeking Prince*), this work, which has been lost to us, tells the story of a young nobleman by the name of San no Miko who searches in vain for the corpse of a lover who has drowned herself and eventually retires from the world and takes the tonsure.

31: Higashiyama, or Eastern Mountains, is historically used to indicate the range of hills east of Kyoto, stretching from Mount Hiei in the north to Mount Inari in the south.

32: The Ryōsen temple, just north of the Kiyomizu temple, was founded by Saichō (766–822). It was later revived by Kokua (1314–1404) as the Shōbō temple, which has survived until today.

33: Following Heian tradition, her stepmother had taken the name after her husband's position, and was still known as Kazusa no Tayū.

34: This scene will be better understood if one remembers that her father was in the street in the midst of his train of attendants—an imposing cavalcade of bowmen, warriors, and attendants of all sorts, with palanquins and luggage, prepared to make a two or three months' journey to the distant province of Hitachi.

35: This was the site of the ancient Kōryū-*ji*, the temple she had visited with her parents sometime before.

36: *Chichi*, in Mount Chichibu, means "father."

37: The custom of the court obliged the court ladies to lead a life of almost no privacy—sleeping at night together in the presence of the empress, and sharing their apartments with each other.

38 *Seri*, in Japanese, and also known as Japanese parsley (*Oenanthe javanica*). There is an old Japanese fable about dropwort: A country person ate dropwort and thought it very fine, so he went up to the capital to present it to the emperor, but the emperor did not like it. So "to gather dropwort" meant to endeavor to win someone's favor by offering something we care for but others do not.

39: The Fujitsubo, the pavilion of the Fujitsubo consort, was one of the buildings housing the empress and the official consorts within the Dairi of the Imperial Palace compound.

40: The *Daijō-sai*, or the Great Festival of Tasting, was the First Harvest Thanksgiving Festival (*Niiname-sai*) of a new emperor—in this case, Emperor Go-Reizai— and part of his enthronement ceremony.

41: In those days it was the custom for the person who wished to be favored by the Inari god to crown his head with a twig of cedar. The Inari god was then the god of the rice plant. He is now confused with the fox-god whose little shrines, flanked by small stone foxes, are seen everywhere.

42 This daughter was most likely the daughter from her husband's previous marriage. The reason for starting from his daughter's house was dictated by directional taboos.

43 The rank of the person determined the color of their clothes. Red was worn by nobles of the fifth degree.

44 It was believed that a *hitodama*, the spirit of a dead person, could be seen leaving the body of someone about to die in the shape of a fiery ball.

45 The name of the place, *oba-sute*, may be translated, "aunt casting away." It is a place famous for the beauty of its scenery in moonlight.

A NOTE ON THE TRANSLATORS

Annie Shepley Ōmori (1856–1943) was an American artist and activist. Having studied art under Harry Siddons Mowbray in New York, and under Jules Joseph Lefebvre and Lucien Simon in Paris, she established her own art studios in New York and Connecticut, where, for the next three decades, she worked as a portrait painter and children's book illustrator.

It was during this period that she met the twenty-years-younger Hyōzō Ōmori, who had come to the United States as a YMCA exchange student. They married in 1907 and together moved to Japan, where they established the Yūrinen settlement house to provide educational and recreational opportunities to the poor in Tokyo. As such they became prominent leaders in the Japanese playground movement.

After her husband's death, in 1913, Shepley stayed in Japan continued running the center. And it was during this period that, together with the Japanese scholar of English literature, Kōchi Doi, she translated the diaries of Murasaki Shikibu, Izumi Shikibu, and Sugawara no Takasue no Musume.

Kōchi Doi (1886–1979) studied English literature and classic Japanese at Tokyo Imperial University. Following his graduation, he did research in France, England, and Italy. On his return to Japan he taught at a number of universities, introducing the English romanticism of James Joice, D.H. Lawrence, and Aldous Huxley. He also pursued his study of classical Japanese literature, the comparative study of mythology, as well as Eastern and Western literature. In 1949, after a distinguished career of various professorships, he became a member of the Japan Academy.

Amy Lawrence Lowell (1874–1925) was an American poet. Born into a wealthy Boston family, she was the sister of astronomer Percival Lowell, educator and legal scholar Abbott Lawrence Lowell, and early activist for prenatal care Elizabeth Lowell Putnam. She was the great-grandchild of John Lowell.

Though she did not enjoy a formal education herself, Lowell was a voracious reader and traveler. And it was whilst in Europe that, in 1902, she saw a performance by the Italian actresss Eleonora Duse, and was inspired to become a poet, publishing her first collection in 1912 under the title *A Dome of Many-Colored Glass*. That same year, she traveled to England with her partner, Ada Dwyer Russel, to come under the spell of the Imagist movement of the expatriate American poet Ezra Pound.

An inveterate smoker of cigars, Lowell died in 1925 of a cerebral hemorrhage. One year later she was posthumously awarded the Pulitzer Prize for Poetry.

HEIAN COURT HEROINES
The abridged *Genji monogatari*
Murasaki Shikibu

TOYO PRess

Explore Dream Discover

Editorial supervision: William de Lange.
Book and cover design: Chōkei Studios.
The typefaces used are Cardo and Forum.
Printing and binding: IngramSpark.